WHAT KIDS WANT
—AND NEED—
FROM PARENTS

"The essential leadership role of parents in any family is to be a mentor for the children, always holding standards high. Joe Gauld has captured all the elements necessary to build strong, deep and lasting bonds between parents and children. If you want to lead your children to a life of purpose and excellence, start with this book."

—Warren Bennis, Distinguished Professor of Management, University of Southern California, and Bestselling Author

*"While my family's three years at Hyde was a struggle, it forced me to open my eyes and eventually it changed my life. Our role as a parent and mentor is to draw out and demand our children's best. It requires that we make the same demand of ourselves, and there are powerful obstacles. Joe Gauld uses his family and other Hyde families as case studies that show us how to overcome these obstacles and establish meaningful bonds with our children. I've said many times that the world would be a better place if we all had the benefit of a Hyde experience. A good place to start is to absorb the wisdom in **WHAT KIDS WANT —AND NEED—FROM PARENTS**."*

—Robert Krebs, Former CEO, Burlington Northern Santa Fe RR

"Gauld offers an exciting paradigm shift of parenting. As a Hyde parent, I have learned that there is nothing more powerful in my parenting repertoire than to role-model the very principles of excellence that I wish most for my children. In my practice as a psychotherapist of forty years, I have incorporated many of Gauld's concepts which have helped transform the lives of thousands of people looking for more fulfilling lives for themselves and their children."

—Caree Brown, LCSW

"This is a book for all parents and future parents, an intimate story of a family and many parents who found out how to connect with their kids. Initially challenging, but in the end, very, very fulfilling. The repeating values in this book—trust, courage, integrity and excellence—are critical for all aspiring leaders and the foundation of the best in our society. Joe Gauld's life is an amazing story of a successful entrepreneur, leader, and educator. His eyes bring out the truth."

—Lennox Black, Former CEO, Teleflex Inc.

"Following Hyde principles helped our family significantly. We learned to set the bar high, hold onto honesty and be the example as we work towards our potential. Thanks Joe Gauld."

—Alvaro de Molina, Former CFO, Bank of America

"As a Hyde School parent for five years, I can personally attest to the power of the family program. Joe Gauld's positive impact on so many lives is legendary. In this book you will find the keys for successful parenting that will result in healthy, long-lasting, and deeply meaningful relationships with your children. A must read!"

—Judith von Seldeneck,
Founder and CEO, Diversified Search

"Today more than ever before, experts understand the overriding primacy of emotional dispositions to student outcomes. A smaller, but still significant number, has grasped that student dispositions are largely determined by those of their parents. But only Joe Gauld has realized, tested and proved that the essential requirement for rapid and lasting student character development and scholastic improvement is parents who are diligently working to improve their own emotional intelligence. Through this indispensable book you'll be inspired and empowered to do the most satisfying soul-work of your life, with the promise that you and your kids will be smarter, happier and more loving."

—Raz Ingrasci, President,
Hoffman Institute Foundation

How to Bond With and Mentor Children

WHAT KIDS
WANT
–AND NEED–
FROM
PARENTS

Joseph W. Gauld

pBook ISBN 9780786754267
eBook ISBN 9780786754274

Distributed by Argo Navis Author Services

Distributed by
Argo Navis Author Services
www.argonavisdigital.com

CONTENTS

This book is a tribute to the rich experience and wisdom I gained from having the privilege of knowing Hyde families at a very deep level —which includes my own family.

Introduction

If you are raising children, are you finding the experience the hardest, most challenging, yet most deeply fulfilling and greatest growing experience of your life?

Today, excellence in parenting and family in America is hard to find. The fundamentals of parenting that nature provides have largely been submerged in an avalanche of advice about how to raise children. The advice may seem appealing and sound right to a particular parent, but the many varying ideas usually end up further confusing the parent-child bond provided by nature.

Over my sixty years as a teacher, it has been painful to experience the continual decline of American parenting and the American family. *Philadelphia Magazine* last year plastered its cover with the words of its lead story: **THE WORST PARENTS EVER!**

It seems the harder American parents try, the worse child-rearing gets. A decade ago, they were criticized for being "helicopter" parents, hovering over the progress of their kids. Today many have earned the title of "snowplow" parents, seeking to eliminate whatever they feel stands in the way of their kids' success.

The tragedy is their efforts are often counter to how nature is asking them to parent. As the saying goes, "Don't mess with Mother Nature."

As a prime example, a big concern of many parents today is ensuring that their children are "happy." Therapist Lori Gottlieb wrote of her own realization of this truth in an article in *Atlantic Monthly*:

Imagine a bright, attractive 20-something woman with strong friendships, a close family, and a deep sense of emptiness. She had come in, she told me, because she was "just not happy." And what was so upsetting, she continued, was that she felt she had nothing to be unhappy about. She reported that she had "awesome" parents, two fabulous siblings, supportive friends, an excellent education, a cool job, good health, and a nice apartment. She had no family history of depression or anxiety. So why did she have trouble sleeping at night? Why was she so indecisive, afraid of making a mistake, unable to trust her instincts and stick to her choices? Why did she feel "less amazing" than her parents had always told her she was? Why did she feel "like there's this hole inside" her? Why did she describe herself as feeling "adrift"?

Gottlieb continues:

I started getting more patients like her. Sitting on my couch were other adults in their 20s or early 30s who reported that they, too, suffered from depression and anxiety, had difficulty choosing or committing to a satisfying career path, struggled with relationships, and just generally felt a sense of emptiness or lack of purpose—yet they had little to quibble with about Mom or Dad.

They truly did seem to have caring and loving parents, parents who gave them the freedom to "find themselves" and the encouragement to do anything they wanted in life. Parents who had driven carpools, and helped with homework each night, and intervened when there was a bully at school or a birthday invitation not received, and had gotten them tutors when they struggled in math, and music lessons when they expressed an interest in guitar (but let them quit when they lost that interest), and talked through their feelings when they broke the rules, instead of punishing them ("logical consequences" always stood in for punishment). In short, these were parents

*who had always been "attuned," as we therapists like to say,
and had made sure to guide my patients through any and all
trials and tribulations of childhood. As an overwhelmed parent
myself, I'd sit in session and secretly wonder how these fabulous
parents had done it all.*

Gottlieb struggles to understand what went wrong and finally
has an "aha!" moment when she realizes, *"Was it possible these
parents had done too much?"* She then begins to research this
question, which ultimately leads to this article entitled: *How to
Land Your Kid in Therapy: Why the obsession with our kids' happiness may be dooming them to unhappy adulthoods.*

We have two major responsibilities with our children: teaching them to respect their best and making them self-sufficient
by roughly age 19. If we do too much for them, we will fail on
both responsibilities, which is revealed by the problems Gottlieb's
patients are having in life.

Clearly, the parents of Gottlieb's patients are not primarily concerned with these responsibilities; they are primarily concerned with their children's happiness. Their children, reading
their parents' hearts, knew this initially, but loving them, couldn't
bear the pain of this truth, and simply went through childhood
and life ignoring it. In time, they eventually forgot it, so they were
honestly able to indicate to Gottlieb they had caring and loving
parents, and honestly didn't know what was wrong with them.

But kids know they need someone who will demand their
best. They fight it because they fear their best may not be good
enough. But it always is.

*

Are you satisfied with your relationships with your children? How
deep are they? If your teenager had a serious personal problem,
would s/he share it with you?

Sadly, in our society teenagers generally share their personal problems with close friends—and more likely they don't share at all. The tragedy is that we adults have yet to understand the profound significance of this deep lack of trust between parent and child in our culture.

There exists a parental instinct to prepare a child for life; as children grow, parents rely on that instinct. Without interference, a parent-child bond will form, and the child will perceive the parent as a mentor, much the way we would depend upon a trusted guide on a difficult journey.

The truth is few families have that relationship today. Why?

One major reason is that we wrong-headedly allowed our achievement culture to dominate our schools when our schools should be committed to the productive growth of children.

This tragic choice paints a picture of our children not as unique individuals, but primarily as students in competition. At a party, when asked about our kid, we would first describe Johnny in terms of his academic achievements or lack thereof (a straight A student; an honor roll student; an underachiever; one who has a learning disability, etc.)

We don't realize we have blindly bought into the rigid mental construct that primarily defines Johnny's self-worth in competition with others in a single arena.

If we had instead responded with what a great artist, musician, athlete, outdoorsman, etc., Johnny is, the listener would probably conclude that Johnny wasn't much of a student in school. That is how entrenched we are in an achievement culture, the prime interference in deep parent-child trust.

We need to ask, what effect does this have on the kids themselves? It is far more disturbing than we realize.

Our children spend thirteen years in school—seventeen if they go to college—where they are continually graded in comparison to their classmates in terms of their academic achievement. While their attitude and effort can significantly help them, they know their ultimate comparison is based on measures beyond their control because, as they know, some students have more natural ability than others.

They are playing in a game that is rigged from the start, on a field that is not level. Thus they develop a "public self" to cope with the realities of the situation, while keeping to themselves a "private self" that contains the deeper emotions about how they feel about all this, which they seldom acknowledge, even to themselves. But those deeper emotions directly affect how they conduct their lives and how they deal with others. This includes us, who urge them on in a game that is rigged.

So how do we handle their unwillingness to share their "private selves" with us? Many parents today, intent on developing close relationships with their offspring, are like misguided teachers who seek to make friends with their students. This desire undermines the deeper bond of trust parents need in order to serve as lifelong mentors for their children.

Children's deepest instincts drive them to seek those who can draw out their best and help them be self-sufficient by roughly age nineteen. This book teaches parents how to do that. It's more challenging than most people realize. But it's never too late.

*

What Kids Want—and Need—From Parents is about how to create the deep bond that nature intended between parent and child.

Children of all ages have capabilities of evaluating their parents' motivations. As you will learn in this book, they read our hearts. So they often know our true intentions better than we do.

This deep bond gives children confidence in a parent's mentorship until they are able to assume responsibility for their own growth. It enables children to absolutely trust that parents place their child's preparation for life above all the other commitments and interests—even above the relationship.

I'm sorry to say most parents and families today are not utilizing this deep bond. They may achieve love, lifetime relationships, loyalty, fondness, and other positive connections, but they are not mentoring the children to become all they were meant to be in life.

Most parents begin with the right dedication to create the bond, but today's parents face heavy outside pressures. The family support system—extended family, neighborhood, church, community services, etc.—has severely eroded. Our achievement culture has undermined the values of the family culture. A media-driven youth culture and commercial interests, empowered by technology, further pull young people away from their parents.

Without realizing it, parents are forced to make accommodations with the achievement culture —or buy into it so they are not "left behind" in their children's world.

And beyond these pressures, there is an even bigger problem. We parents are unaware that our desire to ignore or forget the painful side of our own childhood seriously undermines our bonding with our children.

Sigmund Freud said we are forever changed by the traumas of our youth. We all experience traumas in childhood; it's just a matter of degree. I will share with you later the grim consequences in life of a cross section of 17,000 Americans resulting from their "adverse childhood experiences."

We are on two different wavelengths within ourselves.

Dr. Keith Ablow's thoughtful book, *Living the Truth*, (Little Brown 2007), asks us to face the pain of our childhood as a means to transform our lives "through insight and honesty." The Hoffman Institute, with organizations in twelve countries, helps participants transform their lives by transcending the "negative love syndrome" they internalized in childhood.

No matter how great our parents, they are imperfect people, and as you will learn in this book, as children we internalized their negative patterns—attitudes, behaviors, moods, biases—just as we did their positive qualities.

We deeply love our parents, so we don't want to see or remember them in a negative way. *Our mind may ultimately forget, but our heart (emotions) remembers—as does our spirit.* We are on two different wavelengths within ourselves.

Given this inner head-heart conflict, plus the outside pressures of our achievement society, there may be confusion within us, whether we realize it or not. But our children are not confused. This is their life, and they are totally dependent upon our mentorship. The extent to which we are able to screen out our negative patterns and outside influences is the extent to which they trust us.

My concern for what kids *really* want and need from their parents began fifty years ago, when I made a commitment to change American education. I was determined to find a better way to prepare American kids for life. My focus then was on trying to change American schools.

I founded the Hyde School in Bath, Maine, in 1966 as a model that would refocus the educational process on the premise that every individual is gifted with a unique potential, which I sought to support with a new curriculum based on the development of character—Courage, Integrity, Concern, Curiosity, and Leadership. I believed—and still do—that a primary focus on the development of unique potential and character would solve America's educational problems. Today we have a Hyde network of seven private and public schools focused on this concept.

In the process of developing this better way, I discovered it was even more important to change American parenting than it was to change American schools.

There is a condition that is universally understood. Every child is unique; no one like each child has ever appeared before, or ever will appear again. So as parents, we have a responsibility to draw out the best in each child, and help each child respect the best in him/herself in order to make a unique contribution to life.

> **I discovered it was even more important to change American parenting than it was to change American schools.**

My years of helping thousands of parents and families have taught me a profound respect for the efforts of parents to prepare children for life. From personal experience as well as from the wisdom of others, I know we can achieve a high level of parenting and family excellence in our society today.

You may find some concepts in this book contrary to conventional child-rearing wisdom. I ask you to keep an open mind. I believe you and your child will end up communicating from your heart and soul.

CHAPTER 1

My Story

I believe nature dictates the roles for parents and children. The farmer milks the cows and plants the fields according to nature's plan. Just as placing nature's dictates above the farmer's own desires is essential to his success as a farmer, so is placing nature's dictates for the growth of children above our own desires essential to our success as parents.

We may desire to make our children happy, and for them to be happy all the time, but nature dictates that we prepare them for life, which inevitably involves challenge, adversity, and struggle. They are going to experience life's consequences like uncertainty, failure, and unhappiness along with experiencing confidence, success, and happiness.

On the surface, I'm an unlikely discoverer of nature's parenting process. My educational background is a bachelor's degree in economics and a master's in mathematics, and I'm primarily known today as the founder of Hyde Schools. But my story will explain how I ultimately became deeply immersed in learning the powerful process of how nature expects us to raise children.

My journey of discovery began when I graduated from Bowdoin College in 1950. I woodenly followed my classmates in entering business to become rich and famous. But within months, I knew business wasn't what I was cut out to do.

So I stepped back and took an honest look at myself. I loved baseball and writing songs, but wasn't good enough to make either a career. The only thing I excelled at was helping my mother and aunt raise my two younger brothers and two cousins, and then being a counselor at a summer camp. I painfully realized my calling was in teaching.

I was humiliated, thinking "those that can, do; those that can't, teach." I would be stuck with a bunch of kids and never be rich or famous. To soothe my ego, I resolved to be a great teacher so students would come back years later to thank me for making a difference in their lives.

While this resolve was self-serving at the time, it did deeply commit me to the lives of my students. That commitment ultimately transformed my life.

My intense dedication gave me a fine career as a teacher, coach, and administrator. But my commitment to make a difference in the lives of students ultimately led to a crisis of conscience at a New Year's Eve party in 1962.

I had a lot to celebrate that night. The economy was booming; our family finally had our own home after years in boarding-school dormitories. My appointment as assistant headmaster indicated I would soon be heading my own school.

I loved parties, but as the evening developed, I knew something was wrong. My smile was too fixed, I was trying too hard to be sociable, I felt a growing emptiness inside. Finally I couldn't take it anymore and had to get off by myself. I ended up sitting in the dark, on the edge of an empty stage. I could hear the laughter and music below me in the faculty lounge.

I cried for the first time in years, hardly understanding why. I was not drunk. I felt like a maudlin fool; I told myself I was being ridiculous. But for the life of me I could not stop those tears.

Today I understand those tears as part of a process helping to realize my true destiny. By expressing and dealing with our deeper emotions, we enable ourselves to *transcend* them in order to hear our conscience, which I consider today not just the final determiner of right and wrong, but as the compass that leads us on the path of our true destiny.

At thirty-five, I had reached the top of my profession; it seemed I was destined for a headmastership at some prestigious prep school. But my tears began my awareness that I lacked a deeper sense of fulfillment. And now *my conscience was confronting me.*

I realized our educational system was failing to respect the deeper potentials of kids, to truly prepare them for life, and that I was part of that system.

In my calculus class for example, I told a lazy, arrogant, and self-centered fourteen-year-old genius his attitude would crucify him in life. Yet I was giving him my highest grade! Then I told a discouraged Vermont farm boy to ignore the feeling he described to me—"I work twice as hard as everyone else and get half as much out of it."—and trust that his character would someday ensure his goal of becoming a top engineer. Yet I was giving him my lowest grade!

(Years later, the Vermont boy did become a highly respected engineer, while the genius became unemployed in spite of graduating from MIT at age eighteen with an A average.)

That night at the New Year's Eve party I thought about the failure of our educational system to draw out the deeper potential of kids and prepare them for life. The system was not only failing my students, it was failing students everywhere. I shuddered as I realized if it wasn't my responsibility to change the system, then whose responsibility was it?

My Path Changes

I was at a crossroad. The empty feeling in my stomach told me that no matter how successful I might appear, no matter how assured my future as a headmaster, I could not continue on that path. It was as if in the middle of the night, I was plucked out of my comfortable life in a giant game of morality and tagged "it."

I got up and walked back to the party. Now my empty feeling was replaced by a profound inner tension. I knew I had made a New Year's resolution that would ultimately change the course of my life.

Two years later, I accepted the headmastership of Berwick Academy in South Berwick, Maine. I was encouraged that my character-based program brought a new spirit to the school, but I soon realized I was envisioning change beyond what the school's trustees would accept. Rather than compromise the program, I resigned after a year.

I was proud of the way I stood by my principles, but totally at sea as to what to do next. Another headmastership seemed fruitless, because my experience at Berwick confirmed I was envisioning change beyond what the system could or would accept. Founding a new school without resources or experience seemed foolhardy. If I failed, how would I provide for my family?

But conscience is a powerful force, and my spiritual motivation overcame my fears and concerns. I committed myself to found a new school, and with loans from three brothers and my best friend, donations from three Hyde family heirs, and help from some local citizens who became trustees, I was able to purchase the stately Hyde mansion on one hundred and forty-five wooded acres in Bath, Maine. Hyde School was born in 1966.

To ensure we reached the deeper potentials of each student, the founding premise of Hyde became: *Every individual is gifted with a unique potential.* I sought to support this with a new curriculum based on the development of character—Courage, Integrity, Con-

> **My spiritual motivation overcame my fears and concerns.**

cern, Curiosity, and Leadership. We were determined to prepare every student for life, a mission that included college placement.

I didn't know if the concept of unique potential would hold weight. But, if we made a total commitment to it, I was convinced it would either work, or lead us to something that did.

To help students develop their deeper potentials we challenged them in many areas—academics, athletics, performing arts, community service, jobs, leadership roles. Ultimately, every student accepted many different challenges—introducing themselves to the student body, speaking at school meetings, singing a solo, helping the elderly or elementary students, making a two-minute speech at graduation, and so on.

We are born unique—no one like us before or ever again. We are gifted with powerful intellectual, emotional, and spiritual potentials. The more we discover and express these potentials, the more we express our unique potential in life, and the more fulfilled we become. It's as simple as that.

The Wisdom of Golf

I had an experience learning to play golf in the early '70s that eventually gave me new insight into the development of unique potential, and ultimately, into the wisdom that is the foundation of this book.

In 1970, my wife, Blanche, gave me a set of golf clubs and a membership to our local club for a Christmas present. At the time I was playing tennis tournaments, but I played primarily on the courts at the school. I suspected Blanche was trying to get me out of my total immersion in the school—and my tendency to throw my racket when I didn't like the way I was playing.

In typical fashion, I challenged golf head on. I devoured Ben Hogan's classic book, *Five Lessons: The Fundamentals of Golf.* I hit plastic balls in the snow, and then in the spring practiced playing on our local course at five o'clock in the morning so I could still be at school before eight.

I started out scoring over 100, but set a goal to break 80. A friend bought me six lessons with a golf pro, who began to guide my development. The pro later shocked me by casually saying, "It's only a matter of time before you'll break 70!" At the time my best score was 85, but I trusted him and reset my sights.

I worked hard and got into the 70s, and then read a cheap book that had me spending hours hitting short shots to improve my golf swing. The monotony and frustration I experienced in this learning gave way to the excitement of discovering what really powers a golf ball—*centrifugal force!*

Our mind and ego are strong forces in the golf swing. We may want to hit the ball long and also avoid the woods and hazards on the course. Yet if we can simply visualize the shot we want to make, and then trust the swing we have practiced so many times, centrifugal force will respond perfectly to the proper body movements we give it.

But many golfers, seeking to hit the ball long or to control the shot, unwittingly overpower centrifugal force, with poor results. Place a weight on the end of a string and you will see you must swing it in concert with centrifugal force to swing it high. Similarly, an expert golfer swings his club in concert with centrifugal force to achieve maximum force and accuracy. In essence, all his muscles, from fingers to toes, seek to support centrifugal force.

In the next several weeks I played some of the best golf of my life, breaking 70 several times. I experienced what athletes call playing "in the zone."

How Unique Potential Works

It is quite natural for us to try to control our lives, which we do by leaving all of our crucial decisions to our head or intellect. But this leaves us at the mercy of our ego, which obviously isn't always going to make the best choices for our lives. We have a deeper wisdom located in our heart, which today is called our emotional intelligence. As Jean-Jacques Rousseau noted, *"The heart has its reasons of which reason cannot understand."* But our deepest wisdom is in our soul, highlighted by our conscience, which Hyde calls "the compass of our destiny."

In support of this, *The Social Animal* by David Brooks (Random House 2011) maintains our unconscious self is far more powerful than our rational self, and thus is more congruent with who we really are. Our heart and soul potentials may cause us to lose intellectual and ego control, but like centrifugal force in the golf swing, they will put our unique potential more in control of our lives.

Of course, it goes without saying that we apply the same discipline and growth to our heart and emotions as we do to our head and intellect to make all this work. In time, I learned a sequence for the development of unique potential which I call the "Rigor/Synergy/Conscience-centered learning Process."

Rigor represents disciplined learning to get the best out of ourselves; Synergy, reaching a higher best through the help of others—"others can see our best and our unique potential in ways we ourselves cannot"— enables us to get beyond our ego. This opens us up to Conscience-centered learning, empowering us not only to hear our deepest inner voice, but to follow its lead.

Hyde Schools has come to see the relationship of unique potential to destiny as a lifelong journey. It is like a sailboat that continually tacks in the wind, never sailing toward its destination, but always getting closer.

Over the years I realized centrifugal force is the metaphor for unique potential! The golfer, in his ego-fed desire to hit the ball long or to control the flight of the ball, allows his own muscles to overpower centrifugal force, which results in an unsatisfactory shot.

> **I realized centrifugal force is the metaphor for unique potential!**

By the same token, when we allow our egos and not our unique potential to take control of our lives, then we live lives that do not reflect our best—like my going into business in an attempt to be rich and famous. Just as the golfer must learn to train all of his muscles to support centrifugal force in the golf swing, so must we develop not just our intellect but our emotional and spiritual potentials as well, in order to fully realize our unique potential and our best.

*

Our team of teachers and administrators learned much about how character is developed.

First, it is vital to develop a culture in which students help each other and take responsibility for each other's growth. It is ridiculous to have just adult-run schools. Students taking more of a partnership role make both students and schools more powerful.

So when I founded Hyde, I was determined to have the kids take a leadership role in the school. The key to this was Brother's Keeper—students taking responsibility for each other's best.

This was difficult because in our achievement system of education, kids had generally learned only to share and support their public selves. Thus to point out a fault in a peer would be considered an invasion of one's privacy and "none of your business," as well as the "I don't rat on my buddies" morality if it came to reporting a student who had broken the school's ethics.

It took three years to institute the Brother's Keeper morality, where students realized such efforts could help each other achieve their best. It happened when we sent the seniors on a retreat and they wrote personal evaluations of each other when they returned. The evaluations were both honest and insightful.

Our two wrestling captains who had achieved well at Hyde resisted accepting the honest evaluations of their classmates. When I helped one accept them he finally said, "I guess when twenty-four out of twenty-five of your classmates say you are arrogant and defensive, you need to look at yourself." Unfortunately the next day he reported to me, "My Dad said humility is for losers!"

Strongly supported by their parents, the two boys ultimately rejected the evaluations. I told them if that was their choice, we would certify their high school graduation, but we would not grant them a Hyde School diploma, nor have them participate in our graduation exercises. Their parents took the conflict to our board of trustees, but in the end, it was established that the Hyde diploma stood for character development.

After that, the kids began to open up. The next year in "junior seminar," one student stated the issue, "I'll lower my shield when I see other students lowering their shields." So kids began to reach beyond their public selves to begin a deeper relationship where they began to trust each other with their private selves and to help each other reach their best.

The next year we had a huge "bust" where we found 105 of the 117 students had failed to respect the school's honor code, with most failing to honor their Brother's Keeper responsibility of knowing of ethics violations of classmates and failing to deal with them. The situation broke when I called a school meeting to say I felt something was "off" in the school, and asked the students to trust us to help them deal with whatever is happening.

After interviewing every guilty student, we became aware that students had to deal with a drug, alcohol, and sex culture, and we the faculty had our heads in the sand by expecting they could do so without our help.

Here is what those kids taught us: In the '70s, drugs, alcohol, and sex had become an integral part of the youth culture. Several influential students broke the ethics, a subculture developed, this group of "outlaws" swelled as others slipped, and students became afraid to take their Brother's Keeper concerns to the faculty. And, we had naively expected all kids to be able to do the right thing.

Since I had also realized that character was taught by example, I then began faculty seminars, where I informed the faculty we needed to share our lives and struggles, just like the students were sharing in their seminars, so we could better connect with them and gain their deeper trust.

I eliminated expulsion, saying if we expected the kids to honestly deal with drugs, alcohol, and sex, we couldn't kick out the kids they turned in. Instead, we would hold kids accountable while giving them help. Kids might give up on the rigors of Hyde, but we wouldn't give up on them.

I was not prepared for the resistance I received from some of the more experienced teachers. One said, "We're already formed as individuals; the students are still growing." I tried to coax these reluctant teachers along, even allowing them to make their case to the board of trustees. But when I wouldn't relent, a group of five finally visited the chairman of the board one night to either get me replaced or put on a leave of absence.

The next morning the executive committee of the board visited the school and after talking to other senior faculty members, called me in. The chairman said, "Joe, you are the headmaster of this school. If you don't like the commitment of these guys, fire them."

This ended the resistance, and faculty sharing their lives with each other and with the kids became a natural part of being a Hyde teacher. This created a real bond between teachers and students.

Then in 1973, I gave the kids an anonymous questionnaire to help us keep abreast with their thinking. One question I asked was, *If you had a serious personal problem, who would you go to for help?* Eighty-three percent named a Hyde teacher!

While this was reassuring that we had developed a real bond of trust by sharing our lives with our students, I was deeply disturbed that students had not selected their parents, who should have been their heaviest choice. Was Hyde dealing with some issues that really needed to be addressed at home? With this thought in mind, I began to look at the progress of our graduates in life, once they left Hyde, to try to assess the influence of Hyde.

I found that graduates were generally doing well, but sometimes not. It was puzzling. Why was one student, who had struggled at Hyde, taking off in life while another, who had done well, leveling off?

The answer I finally realized floored me. Parents!

I thought back to the in-depth interviews I did of every entering family. When parents on the way out said to me, "I wish this school had been around thirty years ago," those were parents of

My work ultimately depended upon the parents.

kids who were doing well in life, no matter what the kids did at Hyde. However, when parents were what I came to call "fix-it" parents (eg: "We're all right; it's my kid who has problems,") those were parents of kids who were having trouble sustaining in life what we had taught them at Hyde.

It seemed as simple as this: if the growth we were achieving with the student at Hyde was not also being achieved by the parents at home, then it was questionable if the student would sustain that Hyde growth in life. I had thought I could transform any kid; now I had to accept that most of my work ultimately depended upon the parents.

After a funk, I finally said, "Well Joe, if you really want to help kids, help their parents." So in 1974, Hyde changed course, and

The Power of Parents

In 1964, I had set out to find a better way to prepare American kids for life, beginning with the premise that each student was gifted with a unique potential, which I sought to support with a new curriculum emphasizing the development of character.

What I discovered in 1974 was that we could not effectively deal with this deeper level of development of students without also addressing their parents and families; *in character development, parents are the primary teachers and the home is the primary classroom.*

Schools can seldom develop character—or the deeper potentials involving the heart and soul of students—without the real support or involvement of parents. Picture parents arguing with coaches or umpires at athletic contests, with teachers over grades, or with administrators over discipline, and we realize the limitation of the school's authority when it comes to growth issues beyond the academic curriculum.

There is a dramatic scene in the movie *Hoosiers* where the coach drops two players from the team on the first day of practice because of their attitudes, leaving him only five players for the season. But the next day one father, dragging his repentant son back to apologize, reassures the coach he won't have any problems with his son in the future.

It is a classic example of teacher and parent working together to create a higher best in the child. The film is a David vs. Goliath story about a basketball team from a little town in Indiana who prevailed over all teams in the state to win the state title. It is loosely based on little Milan High School winning the Indiana state title in 1954.

Everything we asked and expected of our students—challenging themselves and others, struggling openly, going after their best—we expected the same from our teachers, who were proving daily how character is taught by example. Now we needed to expect the same from parents—our students' primary teachers.

in spite of being a boarding school, we started saying to parents, "We'll help you raise your kids," introducing a new program that addressed parental growth and family issues on a regular basis.

Helping Parents Help Their Kids

Being a boarding school, the program was ragged at first. We focused much of the work on the initial interview, three-day parent weekends in the fall and spring, telephone conferences, and sometimes, conferences at the school.

But slowly a program emerged. We developed a curriculum for parental growth. Parent regions were formed nationally to enable parents to work together monthly with our curriculum under their own leadership, plus an annual local weekend retreat led by a staff member. We expanded the parent weekends to four days, and added a facility to accommodate an annual four-day Family Learning Center (FLC) experience to help parents focus on their own growth, which also involved their Hyde student.

I now shifted my own primary focus from the kids to the parents. I approached my role with the same dedication I had applied in discovering unique potential. To generalize, the more I sought to help parents, the more I saw I needed to help them shift their focus from their kids to their own growth. And to help them, I needed to get them to focus on their own childhood.

> **I needed to help them shift their focus from their kids to their own growth.**

As I helped parents deal with their childhoods, it became clear that many parents had great difficulty letting go of their own parents. To the extent they hadn't let go of their parents, they were

How Parents Were Raised Matters

If we haven't let go of our parents, it is bound to adversely affect our parent-child bond. For example, at one extreme, some of the parents I worked with saw their parents as "saints" or their upbringing as great or "perfect," which often was essentially the way they viewed themselves in raising their children. The other extreme harbored resentment toward their parents, and often tried to raise their children in opposition to the way they were raised.

Not surprisingly, both these groups tend to have problems in raising their children. Since they had not let go of their parents, their childrearing was overly affected by how they were parented. The first group raises their children as they were raised; the second in opposition to that. In either case, they were *raising their child as if the child were themselves.* But children have a unique potential of their own, and will naturally resist and even resent an upbringing that doesn't respect their own uniqueness. The parents had not taken the steps necessary to develop nature's parent-child bond.

I found that parents who were able to let go of their parents—to appreciate all that their parents had done for them while still being able to recognize their parents' imperfections—made much better progress in their relationship with their children, as well as in their personal lives. It reaffirmed a teaching adage I had developed, "Methods don't raise kids; people do." Thus, if we hope to use any methods in raising our children that our parents used in raising us, we must first separate ourselves and let go of our parents, so we can fully respect the unique and creative parent-child bond that nature has designed for us and our children.

Once we are able to let go of our parents, our focus shifts from ourselves to our child. Then should we employ some method from our childhood, our child responds to our parenting, not to our parents' parenting, and our parent-child bond is reaffirmed.

still partly a child, and a child cannot raise a child. Nature's parent-child bond is a very personal and unique relationship.

The more intensely my seminars with parents dealt with the parents' childhood, as well as with their relationship with their children, the more I realized the strong connection between the two. How parents had connected to their parents in childhood not only strongly influenced how they parented and related to their children, but even how they chose and related to their spouse as well!

As parents, we need to have courage to honestly evaluate our upbringing, to acknowledge and appreciate what our parents did for us— and also recognize that as imperfect people, there were areas where our parents were not at their best.

The more effectively we are able to do this, the more we are able to appreciate the deeper spirit rather than the methods that existed in our upbringing. That spirit empowers our parenting and will inspire the spirit of our children.

It is this rigorous work to truly evaluate the strengths and imperfections of our own upbringing that ultimately allows us to continue our family heritage in our parenting, while fully respecting nature's deep parent-child bond.

> **There were areas where our parents were not at their best.**

In the '70s our family program began to attract media attention, and was featured on NBC's *Today Show*, *The Phil Donahue Show*, and *The David Susskind Show*, and later in 1989, on CBS's *60 Minutes* and in 1995 on ABC's *20-20*.

As our family-based character program matured and gained national recognition, I saw my challenge as proving the Hyde concept could also work in public schools. In 1993, the Hyde Leadership Magnet High School was formed for the New Haven, Connecticut public school system. The Hyde Leadership Charter

School in South Bronx, New York, was founded in 2006 and in 2010 the Hyde Leadership Charter School in Brooklyn, New York, was started. There are Hyde programs today in public schools in Maryland and Florida, supported by the Hyde Foundation, whose mission is to bring the Hyde concept to urban schools and communities.

This frees me to focus on what I believe to be the real key to transforming not only American education, but society as we know it today: parenting and the family. If we can restore these institutions, and then help them fulfill the potentials they have never realized, we will create a revolution that will honor 1776.

Chapter 2

Parenting Basics

While nature doesn't tell us what our responsibilities are in raising children, our success depends upon how well we meet them. So what are they?

Prepare Children for Life's Challenges

Life is difficult. We need to prepare our children for success and failure, to value perseverance, struggle, and hard work as an integral part of a meaningful life.

Parents would do well to consider the lesson of the cocoon. The caterpillar must develop wings strong enough to break out of the cocoon; these wings are then strong enough to fly. Cut open the cocoon to eliminate the struggle, and the caterpillar will simply die.

The same lesson applies to humans. It is our job as parents to make sure that our children are challenged and are faced with adversity, obstacles, and even failure, along with advantages, support, fun, and success. This wider and deeper preparation will lead to a genuine sense of confidence and enthusiasm for life.

The Parent Role

We know nature has given us as parents a distinct responsibility with children—prepare them for life. Further, we understand we have a distinct time frame—prepare them by the end of their adolescence, roughly age 19.

We all know the powerful influence parents have on children's lives and research confirms it. Infants begin seeking our love from birth by trying to imitate us, a process that continues through childhood. They not only know they need us for survival, but as they grow, they realize the quality of their lives depends upon us.

If we prepare our kids to accept the primary responsibility for their lives at roughly age nineteen, then we can begin to step back into a rewarding consultant role for the rest of their lives. We will always be the most influential people in our kids' lives; if we are able to let go of primary responsibility when ours are about nineteen, we will then be able to become a valuable supportive—rather than a restraining—force in their adult lives.

So perhaps a good model for us to follow as parents is that of a guide on a long, challenging journey.

Nothing should be allowed to compromise this parenting role because it will create insecurity at a deeper level within the kids. When this parent-as-guide role is well established and trusted by the kids, productive and close relationships within the family will be created.

It might help parents to visualize having two relationships with their kids; first, that of a guide who has the responsibility to steer the children through the long, challenging journey of childhood and adolescence, most of which is beyond their understanding; and second that as a member and leader of a close, fun-loving family. But always make the first the top priority.

Parenting Leadership

If we parents realized how deeply we actually influence our children's lives, we would work much harder to improve ourselves.

As humans we are imperfect people, and while our children from birth imitate our good qualities and values, they imitate our negative patterns as well.

We all have a dark side that can be triggered by a word, mood, event, etc. When our dark side controls us, we are not at our best, and certainly don't want our children imitating us. So we need to recognize when we are in this pattern and what triggers it. We need to learn how to withdraw from our children and others during these times and what steps we need to take to reenter our normal and positive side.

To understand why we have a dark side consider how most of us were raised to high expectations, which are essential to helping us accomplish what we hope to achieve in life. But high expectations always create a tension within us of what we have yet to achieve, and the person we have yet to become. While this tension normally creates a powerful energy to help us improve and progress, we are human, and there are moments when the tension gets to us and we give in to our imperfections.

It is the expression of these imperfections that undermine our best, and then by imitation, our children's best. This book will help parents understand, identify and address these imperfections passed down to them by their parents. This work is critical in developing the parent-child bond, and establishing the parent as a mentor.

The Fundamentals

In years of working with thousands of parents, it became clear to me there were basic parenting fundamentals needed for success. I put my understanding of this in book form: *Nature's Parenting Process: 5 Simple Truths to Empower Our Children* (Hyde Foundation 2010).

My work with parents led me to a troubling comparison:

We humans have made huge strides in developing skilled physicians, engineers, lawyers, plumbers, and other professionals. Because society sought the best in such professionals over the centuries, information was gathered and rigorous systems of training and research were devised. Today these professions constantly improve, with quality ranging from acceptable to exceptional.

However, since child-rearing has never been a competitive commodity, society has chosen to leave this greatest of all human endeavors solely in the hands of individual parents. Short of extreme abuse or neglect, parents, even teenagers, raise children any way they choose. Not surprisingly, no standard of excellence has ever been established, and sometimes the results are atrocious.

> **No standard of excellence has ever been established.**

This laissez-faire attitude by society can have frightening consequences. In Colonial America, two states passed laws allowing parents to kill a rebellious child. In the 1970s, I talked to a Texas parent after he had killed his pot-smoking son, for which he was acquitted by a jury of his peers. He was convinced he had done the right thing.

I believe we parents have a specific contract with nature. Nature presents us with a fully functioning child at birth, then asks us to bring out the child's best while making the child self-sufficient by the end of adolescence. Nature also provides a process for us to accomplish this.

There are five basic truths in nature's parenting process. I summarize them here:

1. Parent with Humility

It takes humility to recognize the dominant role of nature in child-rearing. I have found the most profound wisdom addressing parenting in *The Prophet* by Kahlil Gibran:

Your Children Are Not Your Children

Your children are not your children.
They are the sons and daughters of life's longing for itself.
They come through you but not from you.
And though they are with you yet they belong not to you.

You may give them your love but not your thoughts,
For they have their own thoughts.
You may house their bodies but not their souls,
For their souls dwell in the house of tomorrow,
which you cannot visit, not even in your dreams.
You may strive to be like them,
but seek not to make them like you.
For life goes not backward nor tarries with yesterday.

You are the bows from which your children
as living arrows are sent forth.
The archer sees the mark upon the path of the universe,
And He bends you with His might that
His arrows may go swift and far.
Let your bending in the archer's hand be for gladness,
For even as He loves the arrow that flies,
So he loves also the bow that is stable.

The first stanza reminds us we are but temporary guardians of children, that life itself dictates a larger purpose for their lives.

The second stanza vitally tells us that "life goes not backward," and since our children's souls "dwell in the house of tomorrow," we need to make sure that both we and our parenting search for and respect the uniqueness in our children, including some of their thoughts.

The third makes us realize that we and our parenting are a vital part of a larger plan, and parenting fulfills a larger purpose in life.

This is what I hope parents take away from Gibran's wisdom:

We are assistants to a power beyond ourselves, an acceptance of which empowers us to trust our best efforts in raising our children and then let go of the outcomes.

Both challenging and supporting the development of our children's unique potential will require changes in ourselves and our parenting.

2. Parent beyond Love

King Solomon confirmed a model for the parent-child bond in the story of two women fighting over which one of them is the mother of a child. He directs his swordsman to cut the baby in two, and give each woman half. One woman immediately says, "She's the mother!" Whereupon Solomon recognizes her as the true mother, because her commitment is not to the baby, but to the baby's future.

Fortunately, nature seems to recognize the difficult task given to us as parents. We are presented with highly motivated babies who eagerly want to learn from us!

The first thing infants experience is fear of abandonment—they know they cannot survive without us to take care of them. So they seek our love, feeling if we love them, we will always be there when they need us. How do they seek our love? By imitating us! Amazingly, they instinctively believe if they are like us, we will love them.

Thus we should never seek the love of our children, because it will interfere with the natural order of children seeking our love. Children who realize their parents want their love will no longer feel the need to seek love from their parents—they already have it.

Instead, they can now manipulate their parent by using the parent's desire for their love to get what they want; thus the parent's vital role as a mentor is compromised. And since children learn to read their parents' hearts, this can happen at an early age.

Parents need to discipline their feelings so they can maintain their roles as mentors. In doing so, their children are reassured—usually unconsciously—that the basic purpose in how they are being raised is their preparation for life. This is fundamental to children's deep trust and respect in their caretakers.

The point needs to be emphasized. Children begin life seeking to imitate their parents, because they need caretakers in order to feel secure. So as long as parents are focused on preparing their children for life, their children feel secure and follow their parents'

> **Parents need to discipline their feelings so they can maintain their roles as mentors.**

lead. However if a parent seeks the child's love, the parent wants something from the child, and the child no longer feels that deep sense of security. Instead, the child now has a position of authority.

3. Parent with Principles

Since we have a limited time to prepare our children for life, like a good teacher, we practice "principles over personalities" to keep the focus on what we teach. Since we are all imperfect, we don't want our own shortcomings to define who our children become.

This is illustrated by an episode one morning when our son Malcolm was about three years old:

> *I was late for class, and he had crawled into bed with Blanche, watching me frantically trying to get dressed. I was increasingly frustrated by not finding what I needed, so when I opened the drawer filled with socks, none of which matched, I finally exploded. I started angrily throwing them on the floor: "I wish [throw] I had [throw] two socks [throw] that matched!" Whereupon Mal said, "If you act that way about it, you won't*

get any!" Blanche threw the sheet up over her head, and I stood there like a chastened child.

The story highlights that even at this early age, children are capable of seeing beyond our dominant parental personalities to grasp our principles and values. Since we are imperfect, we must teach our children our principles are their ultimate authority, not us.

Making principles the final authority also avoids unnecessary power struggles with growing children.

Children are constantly testing limits to determine their capabilities; they will inevitably test parents who impose such limits. Even the best of us will sometimes be inconsistent or wrong, which invites any child to challenge parental boundaries. But principles will be the same tomorrow as they are today, leaving children to question parental interpretation of principles,

> **Even the best of us will sometimes be inconsistent or wrong.**

not parents themselves. This allows children to accept parental direction without feeling they are just giving in to our dominant personality and authority.

4. Take Hold as We Let Go

A telephone survey twenty years ago determined that the average parent felt it was okay for offspring to still be living at home at the age of 24, and my experience says it's later now. Clearly, we Americans have difficulty letting go of our children.

We parents today are more focused on our children's success than we are on teaching them to take responsibility for themselves and their development. Too often we interfere in their shortcomings, mistakes, and failures, to the point where they learn to rely upon us and not upon themselves when faced with difficult situations.

In a given situation, we need to first determine and take hold of our responsibility as a parent; this will clarify the responsibility we need to expect from our child.

My daughter-in-law, Laura, who oversees our two Hyde boarding schools, had this childhood experience:

At fifteen, egged on by friends, she took the family car for a joy ride, hit a parked car and left the scene of the accident. When she finally returned home, she was greeted by the police. Her devoted stepfather simply tossed a telephone book to her, saying, "You're going to need a lawyer." Laura had to handle everything, including earning money to pay for damages and the lawyer. Looking back, she considers that moment of letting go from her stepfather to be one of her most important learning experiences.

Her stepfather, a Hyde parent at the time, realized his most important job was to make sure Laura experienced the full consequences of her actions.

We parents should realize that if we don't hold our children responsible for their actions, then we are conveying a lack of confidence in their capability of taking responsibility for themselves.

It is important for us to realize that adolescence in particular is

> **If we don't hold our children responsible for their actions, then we are conveying a lack of confidence in their capability.**

the practice field of life. This is the time when our children should be rigorously challenged, taking risks, discovering themselves, their capabilities, and how to deal with their shortcomings, mistakes, and failures. Someone who completes this kind of "obstacle course" develops a real self-confidence and enthusiasm for life.

5. Parent by Example

Parents are the most powerful figures in our lives. Since we are the child's primary teachers, we are always his/her primary source of learning, even when we are not consciously teaching or parenting. I painfully learned this truth when my oldest child was nine:

> *I noticed Mal's best friend was wearing my old watch. He said Mal had given it to him, but when I confronted Mal, he denied it. Since Mal was the golden boy in town and his friend was in constant trouble, it seemed clear who was lying. But in the confrontation that followed, Mal finally admitted giving his friend the watch! I was thunderstruck. How could Mal allow his best friend to look like a thief?*
>
> *My first thought—did God give us a lemon?—showed me where my ego was. Clearly, I had a problem: if Blanche and I were going to take credit for our wonderful kids, how could we not also take credit for their shortcomings? I knew somehow I had set the example for Mal's blatant dishonesty.*

I became more concerned with my own shortcomings than with my son's.

Once I searched for an example of my dishonesty, I found it. I had always said to Mal, "I don't care how well you do, as long as it's your best." It may have been true in my head, but not in my heart. I was emotionally dishonest; Mal knew I *did* care how well he did. As much as I focused on Malcolm's best, I had to admit that secretly I craved my son's achievements in academics, athletics, and elsewhere.

I was really disappointed in myself. Was I trying to make his life a trophy in *my* life so I could take credit for his achievements? I knew Mal trusted my guidance, and I had seriously let him down. It took time to change this deep attitude in myself toward my son's achievements, but once I did, his lying disappeared.

This episode also points out that children read our hearts, not our minds. So as Mal did here, they often know our real or ultimate intentions better than we do.

Chapter 3

The Foundation of Nature's Parent-Child Bond

Since it really does "take a village to raise a child," I maintain we presently live in a society where it is difficult for any of us to achieve our parenting potential. Our educational system teaches us to be ego-centered, not purpose-centered.

Think about it. Our entire education is centered on us as individuals and our careers. Then we face the difficult challenge of getting out of our egos to learn how to share our lives with our spouses and families. Finally we enter the big leagues when we have to learn to put our children's lives above our own. Our learning process doesn't prepare us or our peers for this profound need for humility, so we essentially may become the blind leading the blind.

If we note the Asian cultural emphasis on family and their success in parenting, I may not be overstating the situation as much as some may think. The excellent book *Leadership and Self-Deception: Getting out of the Box* (The Arbinger Foundation 2000) points out how our egos can lead us into ignoring shortcomings in ourselves as we focus on shortcomings in others. In essence, we then become involved in *self-deception*.

For example, say I am awakened by our crying baby, Timmy. But being very tired, I wait, hoping my wife will wake up to take care of him. When she doesn't, my thoughts begin to remember her shortcomings—how she can be inconsiderate and lazy, maybe she's faking sleeping, waiting for me to wake up.

I'm involved in self-deception. I can get out of this box by simply listening to what my best says: get up and attend to Timmy so my wife can sleep. If I continue to do what my best says, I can stay out of the box. This will lead to a very different relationship with my wife—and to myself.

The same is true with our children. In the last chapter, I shared my first reaction to my son giving away my old watch without my permission and lying about it—what is wrong with this kid?—until I suddenly realized my ego was off-track. Then I started looking at myself, saw my shortcoming, dealt with it, and got out of the box. Eventually Mal's lying went away.

Before we end up with a "Holier than thou" attitude with our kids and even our spouse, we need to take a careful inventory to find the places where we are deceiving ourselves about our own attitudes and deal with them. If we do, we will find our relationships with the family will greatly improve!

So while we were all trained in an educational system that tended to teach us to develop our relationships through our egos, this book will focus us more on the Hyde Rigor/Synergy/Conscience-centered learning process that teaches us how to work with others and do the right thing. This lays the foundation for the parent-child bond.

The Mentor Role: Part of the Bond

Nature's parent-child bond is created by the parent's ability to focus on what children most need in order to become uniquely effective adults. Children, recognizing this ability in parents, accept them as their mentors, thus forming nature's parent-child bond.

Many parents fail to create this bond because while they begin with one-hundred percent responsibility for their child at birth, without understanding, they may either take a too dominant role in determining the parent-child relationship over the years, or simply fail to fulfill the role required of a mentor.

Such approaches fail because nature has programmed our children to ultimately respond to: 1) our efforts to bring out their best and 2) our preparation to enable them to become self-sufficient after adolescence. Nature has endowed us with parenting instincts to accomplish both of these tasks, but our lack of understanding, our egos and other motivations can block the way.

> **Our deepest bond of trust is formed when we help them take responsibility for themselves.**

It is a given that we need to care for our children. But our deepest bond of trust is formed when we help them take responsibility for themselves. These developments, which will last a lifetime, lead them to embrace us as their mentors.

An extraordinary example of a powerful mentor relationship is when Dwight Eisenhower refused to have his leg amputated at age fifteen, when specialists warned his parents it was necessary to save his life. Parents today would feel compelled to direct the surgeons to amputate. But Ike's parents had carefully developed his sense of personal responsibility, and unhappily felt they had to accept that at age fifteen, this had to be his decision, not theirs.

Ike's parents certainly did it the way nature had intended, because it is now very clear Ike needed that leg to fulfill his exceptional destiny as the Supreme Commander of Allied Forces in World War II and then as the thirty-fourth President of the United States. We have the Eisenhowers to thank for raising a very responsible fifteen-year-old who fully knew the consequences of the situation. We can thank them for believing that critical decision had to be between their son and his higher power, in spite of information to the contrary. Obviously in this particular case, fifteen-year-old Ike knew best.

Very few parents today could—or should—allow their children to make such a crucial decision at age fifteen, because most have not prepared their children to take that responsibility.

My wife is an exception. I asked Blanche what she would do if our son Malcolm had refused the amputation at age fifteen, and this was our conversation:

> She: We'd talk about it.
>
> Me: Suppose he still refused?
>
> She (After a pause): Well, we'd talk about it some more.
>
> Me: Blanche, I know you believe you could talk him out of it, but suppose you couldn't?
>
> She (After thinking a long time): It would kill me, but I guess I would have to accept his decision.

I had expected this answer. Blanche was raised on a farm, and had learned a deep respect for nature's leadership, which in turn enabled her to cultivate, and sometimes demand, our children's increasing responsibility for their own growth.

Many parents today are doing too much for their children, "hovering" too much over them, and protecting them too much from risk, failure, and even adversity. Life is deliberately designed to be difficult in order to challenge our deepest and most powerful potentials—it's why we humans usually flourish in adversity, but flounder in prosperity.

It has always been understood that a very deep relationship occurs between a child and his/her primary caregivers, and that this relationship continues to have a powerful influence on the child's life.

This understanding began to take a scientific form with Dr. John Bowlby's attachment theory in the 1950s, which is generally accepted by the psychiatric community today.

Bowlby stated that the infant's attachment to a primary caregiver (usually the mother):

- was essential to the infant's survival and therefore to the continuation of the species
- provided a vital period for the infant's innate sense of attachment to develop
- allowed the infant's innate charms—laughing, crying, even the infant's face itself—to draw out the innate child-rearing potentials from the caregiver
- provided the infant a guaranteed safe base from which to explore and grow
- provided a sound foundation for the infant's emotional growth and self-esteem
- provided a model for the development of the infant's other emotional relationships

Bowlby's list helps us understand and appreciate why primary caretakers are critical to the full development of infants, and ultimately to their development in life. This and later research explains why if a child does not find a caretaker to trust in the first three years of life, it will have difficulty trusting others in life.

This deep need for attachment by the infant led to this understanding:

At birth, infants experience anxiety from the fear of abandonment, knowing they cannot survive without a primary caretaker—usually their parents. Babies seek their parent's love by imitating

> ## Babies seek their parent's love by imitating them.

them, feeling if they are like their parents, their parents will love them, and thus be there when the infants needs them. (Even at birth, infants can identify love with imitating us, suggesting self-love is a basic human drive. If so, we must learn to fully appreciate ourselves, or it will create conflicts with other drives in our lives, consciously or not.)

An important point to recognize here is that children, until age seven or eight, are egocentric, which means they take everything that happens in the family personally. If parents fight or Dad leaves home, children feel it is their fault. Not having their parents' time and attention creates the feeling of being unworthy—the child is not worth his parents' attention and direction. Young children in particular need reassurance, particularly when there are dysfunctions or other distractions in the family.

The Best Self We Can Be

We also need to realize just how children learn to understand us. Since parents are always intellectually well ahead of children, chil-

> ## Children often know their parent's deeper intentions better than parents know them.

dren learn to listen to or read their parents' emotions or heart far more than their parents' mind or words. As a result, children often know their parent's deeper intentions better than parents know them themselves. We are reminded again of Rousseau's quote, "The heart has its reasons of which reason cannot understand."

If a child is to grow properly, its primary commitment must be to doing his/her best and becoming self-sufficient. Helping the child meet this commitment must be the top priority in our life as the parent.

To keep our children's trust and confidence in us as strong as possible, we must always return to the two parental initiatives we need to focus on to cement our parent-child bond: our children's best, and continually preparing for their self-sufficiency by roughly age 19.

Our kids—and all of us for that matter—know the most powerful and durable resource we will have in life is our best, being the best self we can be.

No matter what the situation, if we have been able to give it our best, we always feel a deeper sense of satisfaction and serenity, no matter what the outcome. At the same time, the reverse is true; we feel a lack of fulfillment and dissatisfaction when we don't do our best, even when we succeed.

We rely upon our parents to help us learn what our best is, our true best cannot be achieved without the help of others. As Henry Ford remarked, "My best friend is the one who brings out the best in me."

In the Rigor/Synergy/Conscience stages of growth, the synergy stage is described: *others see our best and our unique potential in ways we ourselves do not.* In addition to teaching us the value of rigor, our parents introduce and sensitize us to this synergistic path to our true best. Synergy gets us thinking beyond our ego and our self-centeredness.

When a family operates well, every member is always concerned about the best in all other members. So we parents first help cement our parent-child bond by becoming consistently effective at recognizing and drawing out our children's best.

In spite of my stepfather's excessive discipline and several times being unfair to me—a difficult situation for a kid to live with—I generally trusted his parenting because he often challenged my best. My friends laughed at some of the chores my stepfather assigned to me. While it was embarrassing, subconsciously, I felt he expected more from me than their fathers were expecting from them. It quietly encouraged my maturity and discipline.

In all our concerns about our kids, helping them realize their best must be our highest priority, which means *we must model for them going after our own best.* If our relationship with them starts to go off-track, we should first ask ourselves if our kids' best and our own are still our top priorities.

We naturally want to be proud of our kids and we may consider, unconsciously or not, how they compare to other kids, academically, athletically, socially, and in other ways. This can easily create tension in our kids, contribute to their lack of confidence, and misguide their development. Remember, kids read our heart even if we don't.

Instead, we should constantly focus on our kids' own best, which makes us effective in evaluating how well they are developing their unique potential. This not only contributes to their self-confidence, but builds their confidence and trust in our parenting as well.

Our kids need our high expectations and high standards. We live in a very competitive society, so we must make sure these expectations and standards relate to their personal best, not in competition with others. We want our kids to learn that while we like to win, our pride is reserved for what reflects an excellent effort. Creating this attitude in our kids takes thoughtful and dedicated parenting.

> **Our kids need our high expectations and high standards.**

Given our many responsibilities in life, our kids' growth and their best can easily slide from being our top priority without our realizing it. But our kids will always realize it, at the cost of their confidence, spirit, and motivation. They know they are a work in progress and they depend upon our vision and commitment for their fulfillment.

Growing up, I felt the only thing I really had going for me was my mother's belief in me. I didn't know what she saw in me, but I knew she saw something, and I trusted her. That helped me believe somehow life would ultimately work out for me.

To ensure that kids are always primary in our lives, we need to focus on their best, not only if they are doing their best, but also if they are engaged in activities that challenge their true best.

Holding to High Standards

I think a standard for realizing the best in American children was set when Anne Sullivan took over the development of nine-year-old deaf, blind, and mute Helen Keller. In a famous breakfast scene, Anne dismissed Helen's entire family so she could fully deal with Helen's attitudes as the first step in demanding Helen's best.

At first Helen angrily rebuffs Anne's relentless attempts to help achieve her best, but in time accepts her as her mentor. Anne became known as the "Miracle Worker," and we know Helen today as one of the outstanding individuals of the twentieth century.

I recently read *Battle Hymn of the Tiger Mother* by Amy Chua (Penguin Press 2011) Chua describes her week of struggles in trying to help her daughter Lulu master a very difficult piece on the piano:

I used every weapon and tactic I could think of. We worked right through dinner into the night, and I wouldn't let Lulu get up, not for water, not even to go for the bathroom. The house became a war zone, and I lost my voice yelling, but still there only seemed to be negative progress, and even I began to have negative doubts.

Then, out of the blue, Lulu did it. Her hands suddenly came together—her right and left hands each doing their imperturbable thing—just like that ... that night she came to sleep in my bed, and we snuggled and hugged, cracking each other up.

Chua's Chinese-style parenting is much too much for most American parents. But while we may find fault with some of her methods, we need to recognize she is giving her kids a powerful resource in their lives—a strong belief in their best to prevail under the most difficult conditions. In her words:

Western parents worry a lot about their children's self esteem. But as a parent, one of the worst things you can do for your child's self esteem is to let them give up. On the flip side, there's nothing better for building self-confidence than learning to do something you thought you couldn't.

I had some of that in my own home growing up.

My stepfather not only assigned chores for me that he then inspected, but he sought ways to challenge me. For example, not liking my vocabulary, he once assigned a two hundred-fifty word essay in which I couldn't use the verb "to be" (try that sometime.) My mother signed me up for piano lessons and tap dancing lessons where I was the only boy in the class!

I grew up in a dysfunctional household where both parents were un-recovering alcoholics, with my mother ultimately going insane. But the power of their commitment to our best sustained my and my siblings' growth until we were old enough to recognize that her drinking was beyond her control. In my stepfather's case, it was only after we left home that we recognized he was a functioning alcoholic.

These family dysfunctions did cause problems that we needed to deal with in life. But the constant focus on our best and the preparation to make us self-sufficient gave us an independence to pursue our unique potentials..

Our kids depend upon us to prepare them to be self-sufficient by roughly age 19.

Many kids approaching maturity will profess, or even believe, they are ready to run their own lives at age fifteen or so. This is partly why the preteen and teen years often involve a tug-of-war with kids seeking more freedom and responsibilities, while parents feel the need to stress accountability and the earning of privileges.

In this tug-of-war, there is a letting-go process that is very difficult on both parent and kids, but it is the ultimate bonding experience.

Who's Taking Responsibility?

Kids have a natural fear of growing up (often called the Peter Pan Syndrome.) Kids don't have confidence they can convert their childhood dreams into reality. So if their parents don't carefully prepare them throughout their childhood to slowly take responsibility for their own lives, they will naturally tend to hold on to their parents in life.

Parents today have a tendency to try to protect kids when they experience negative outcomes. Instead, they should consider approaching some of these negatives experiences as important opportunities to help their kids learn to take responsibility for their lives.

Think back to what I wrote earlier about my daughter-in-law Laura, who at age 15, took the family car without permission and hit another car. Her stepfather made her take full responsibility for the episode, and it became one of the most important growth experiences of her childhood.

We Americans are not doing a good job of preparing our kids to be self-sufficient. I can remember when our son Malcolm graduated from Bowdoin, and Blanche and I drove him and all his belongings to his first teaching job in New York. As we drove out of the school grounds, Blanche wiped her eyes as she said, "Well, that's that!"

Painful as it was, she meant it. Then we began a new relationship with Mal where he valued us as a pair of trusted consultants as he began to become head of his own household.

Unfortunately, this formal changing of the guard in families is the exception rather than the rule. In dealing with thousands of parents, I find very few have truly let go of their own parents, as Mal did. Instead they are still in the parent-child relationship to some degree, which means they are not fully head of their own households. This is not healthy for children or for their parents.

Taking hold always precedes letting go. Taking hold means to first determine one's own responsibility in a relationship, and then let go of the rest of the responsibility to the other person.

Many problems are caused in parenting because the parent becomes too preoccupied with what the kid is or is not doing. Taking hold means to first determine what we should do as parents, take hold of that, then let go, and firmly insist our kids take hold of their responsibility. Continue repeating this process, and kids will not only understand the concept of responsibility, but eventually appreciate the process of being prepared for self-sufficiency.

The first time parents become determined to hold their kid accountable after rescuing him/her a number of times will be the hardest, perhaps almost unbearable. But if parents can weather that storm, life gets better, and so does their kid.

Parents are naturally concerned about their children's safety. But their deeper parent-child bond through nature enables them to endure their kid's pain and fear in order to prepare their child to be self-sufficient by age 19. Those struggles are a vital part of the learning process, and lead to a powerful feeling of accomplishment and self-confidence.

> **The first time parents become determined to hold their kid accountable after rescuing him/her a number of times will be the hardest.**

Let me use a dramatic Hyde example to illustrate the importance of taking hold and letting go in parenting, as well as the deep insight of kids into the hearts of their parents:

Hyde parents and students both make a commitment at the interview to participate and complete their respective programs. In the 1980s, two new sixteen-year-old girls who had difficulty with the rigors of the Hyde program decided to run away. I received a call from the local chief of police, "Joe, I know your policy at Hyde of not pursuing a runaway, but these two girls are in with some very bad characters." I thanked the chief and immediately reported to the girls' mothers what the chief had said, while still advising both of them not to interfere, and to hold firm to the commitment they made at the interview.

But one mother came, grabbed her daughter and placed her in a mental hospital. However, the other mother took my advice and didn't interfere. Shortly after, her daughter returned to school. Several months later, I was next to her in the lunch line and said, "Mary, you've done a great job ever since you came back; how did you make such a miraculous change?" Mary simply said, "I knew my mother meant it." Mary went on to graduate as a school leader.

There is an important lesson here. Mary knew her mother was probably sick with worry, not just over her running away, but with the company she was keeping. But she also knew her mother is committed to her. So she realized her mother was essentially saying, "If this is what our relationship means to you, then there's nothing I can do." Mary realizes she is losing something very important to her, and she must step up not just to regain the relationship with her mother, but for her own life as well. She took a vital step in learning personal responsibility, while re-establishing a bond with her mother.

Mary's episode at Hyde occurred more than thirty years ago. Today she is a parent and maintains a great relationship with her mother. In retrospect, Mary's behavior was a case of a mother's love blinding both mother and daughter to the magic of nature's parent-child bond, with Mary not living up to her responsibilities of growth, and her mother unwittingly overly protecting her. Hyde served to help them reestablish nature's bond.

Mary's teenage transformation reaffirms for us that kids are capable of deep insights into their parents, because of their ability to read their parents' hearts.

Children Have a Deep Understanding

As an example of how deeply kids can read their parents' hearts, my 1962 crisis of conscience was a deeply spiritual experience for me that I didn't share with anyone, even my wife, until I wrote about it thirty years later. But incredibly, through a paper he wrote eight years later, I discovered my ten-year-old son Malcolm was aware of my transformation:

I can well remember when my father was just a regular teacher in a regular school. What stands out most clearly was his deep desire to be a headmaster, inquiring about schools as far away as the west coast.

I didn't then perceive my father as having any unique ideas for bettering American education. In fact, I envisioned him as maintaining the traditional form, setting up shop with us as the 'first family' on some campus.

When I was around ten, it looked as though my father would land a headmastership in Florida. Pops was so excited over the prospect he could barely control himself. I tried to fake enthusiasm; after all, I was proud he was going to be a head-master. But I shuddered at the very idea of leaving rural New England.

Then, right after returning from Florida, Mom and Dad had one of their 'serious' conversations in the living room. Their expressions told me we wouldn't be moving to Florida. I heard them use some big sounding words. The word that stuck out was segregated—the reason that Dad refused the job.

I was so proud of my father for refusing to work at a school that wouldn't admit blacks, I bragged about it to all my friends. I don't know if they understood my enthusiasm, but I didn't really care.

Perhaps my father believed all this slipped over my head or perhaps he didn't view it as a major decision on his part. But I needed that example. I liked being the son of the head coach, teacher, administrator, but that image had a hollow ring. It was his losing the Florida job that gave me something I could really understand, look up to, and follow.

(I should add the year was 1964, when some private schools were still segregated, both north and south.)

At age ten, it is amazing how well Malcolm read me through my emotions. I did deeply want a headmastership, and if it had been fifteen months earlier, before my crisis of conscience, I might have accepted the trustees' stated desire to integrate the school. As it was, when it seemed we had an agreement, I bluntly said, "Look, I'll work with you on integrating the school. But if you don't fully intend to integrate, then don't hire me." My New Year's Eve commitment had changed my primary focus, and Malcolm had understood this without our ever discussing any aspect of it.

This chapter sought to explain how much our children depend upon us to prepare them for life, and the depth of their insight into us as their mentors.

Now that we understand the foundation of the parent-child bond, we will need to understand the biggest roadblock to its development, which undermines our growth and our children's as well: negative childhood experiences passed down to our family by our parents, and passed down to them by their parents.

Chapter 4

The Deepest Roadblock to the Bond

We know our kids deeply depend upon us both for their survival and preparation for life, so they seek to imitate us to get our love in order to ensure we will both protect them and prepare them for life. Chapter 3 showed us how this imitation strategy enables kids to understand us at a deeper level by reading our emotions or heart, sometimes deeper than we understand ourselves.

We parents in turn grow to deeply love our kids, whose lives we put above our own and whose preparation for life becomes our top priority.

Given this powerful two-way bond, why do we have so many parent-child struggles and family dysfunctions today? Don't we both want the same thing?

The basic problem is we parents do not really understand the role that nature intends and that our kids expect us to take in their growth. Our kids need us to mentor them over those first nineteen years. They know they need mentors who will draw out and even demand their best.

This is why I was able to tolerate my stepfather's constant criticism and the several times he was unfair, which I chalked up to his jealousy of my closeness to the woman he loved. But ultimately, I trusted he was an honorable man who was determined to raise my brother and me properly, whether we liked it or not.

Kids Know When Parents Demand Their Best

Kids have this deeper insight. They can see how well their parents are demanding their best and saying "no" to them, particularly compared to other parents.

Coming from strong, high-expectation families, they often see their parents caught in the conflict between the values of the family vs. the values of the achievement or youth culture. Parents, dealing with the realities of life, seldom realize the compromises being made between these two conflicting value systems. But their kids do, as somewhat reflected in their indulgence in drugs, sex, and other forms of rebellion.

Many kids come to accept the situation for what it is, simply going into life building upon the many strengths they internalized in their family, while ignoring the unrecognized compromises being made, which often compromise their spirit.

Some kids become rebels who choose to act out the compromise. This forces a moment of truth in the family. If parents see this only as the kid needing help, then the kid will probably continue a rebellious off-track path, unless the kid ultimately decides to conform to a more acceptable path that probably doesn't reflect his/her spirit.

> **Acting out is generally a cry for help.**

It has been our experience at Hyde that the acting out is generally a cry for help, not just for the kids, but for their families as well, that in effect, these kids are acting as the conscience of the family in trying to force it to change in some way, to get the help it needs. This is an *unconscious* motivation on the part of these rebellious kids. They are reacting to nature's parent-child bond of needing a mentor to be prepared for life, knowing at this deeper level this is not happening for either them or their siblings.

At Hyde Schools, eighteen administrators today are Hyde School graduates; of these, about one-third were rebels who were off-track in their own lives, but in their acting out, they were forcing both themselves and their families to get help.

They all came from solid families whose high expectations allowed the family values to be slowly infiltrated by the values of today's achievement culture, as well as problems passed down from their families of origin (to be discussed.) So in time, the emphasis in the family became harmony over truth, with family issues and problems not being dealt with. The parent-child bonds and mentorship roles had become submerged, if not lost.

It is interesting to note that while both parents and student in such families changed at Hyde, the transformation of the student usually occurred *after* the transformation of the parents.

But more than the negative pressure on the family from our achievement culture and the loss of the family support system, there is an even deeper problem that exists in virtually all families that undermines the parent-child bond and our mentorship role.

This problem is not widely recognized and is seldom addressed. Thus, it has become the biggest roadblock to the development of the parent-child bond, and to the parent role as a mentor.

Our society is largely unaware of:

- how human imperfections are transmitted from parent to child during childhood
- the disruptive power these imperfections have on human growth

- how deeply, if unaddressed, these imperfections affect the next generation

The most powerful way our children develop character, values and a sense of purpose is by imitating us. But the intense imitation process has a down side. Since we are imperfect people, our

> **The intense imitation process has a down side. Since we are imperfect people, our children also internalize our negative patterns.**

children also internalize our negative patterns—our unproductive attitudes, behaviors, moods, and biases.

Our negative patterns are not in our genes; we internalize them in our attitudes, behaviors, moods, and biases through the imitation process. If they are not addressed, they are passed down from generation to generation. Raising children makes us better people, but our negative patterns will still undermine our best efforts.

These negative patterns are deeply internalized in our emotions. As much as we may try to control them, under pressure, our emotions will at times overwhelm our rational mind. Much as we may hate to admit it, it is like we caught a virus from our parents, and we can't prevent our children from catching this virus from us.

The Impact of Adverse Childhood Experiences

A 1998 Adverse Childhood Experience (ACE) Study shows how the negative patterns internalized in childhood not only compromise adult lives, but also the lives of our children.

This is how the study originated: Dr. Vincent Felitti of Kaiser Permanente, one of the authors of the study, initially set out to help obese people lose weight. Felitti learned that many had been unconsciously using obesity as a shield against unwanted sexual attention, or as a form of defense against physical attack, and that many of them had been sexually and/or physically abused as children. So while obesity was conventionally viewed as a problem, to the patient it was an unconscious solution to a deeper and more concealed problem.

At the same time, Dr. Robert Anda of the Centers for Disease Control was studying multiple medical and public health problems including smoking, alcohol abuse, obesity, and chronic diseases. So the two physicians developed a common interest in doing a major study on the influence of childhood experience on health and welfare later in life.

Studies Confirm Impact of ACE

Confirming the power of adverse childhood experiences, in 2005, the National Institute of Mental Health found 46.4 percent of Americans meet the standard for a mental disorder, and that half reach it by age twelve.

Further, according to a 2009 Gallup-Healthways Well-Being Index, 63.1 percent of Americans are overweight, of which 26.5 are obese.

In addition to obesity, the most common health risks today are smoking, alcohol, illicit drug use, and sexual promiscuity. All of these are directly correlated to ACEs.

To give you some idea of the scale, compared to those who had an ACE score of 0, the study found that those with an ACE score of 4 (out of 10) were twice as likely to smoke, seven times more likely to be alcoholic, 10 times more likely to be a street drug user and 12 times more likely to have tried suicide.

It gets worse. Those with an ACE score of 6 vs. those with a score of zero were 44 times more likely to be suicidal and 46 times more likely to be a street drug user.

As for sex, those with an ACE score of four were four times more likely to have intercourse by age fifteen, twice as likely to experience teen pregnancy, and three times more likely to have more than fifty sexual partners, than those with a score of zero.

The study also related actual diseases to adverse childhood experiences, particularly to alcohol, tobacco, and stress. They found those with a score of 4 were twice as likely to have liver disease, twice as likely as having lung (COPD) disease and at least 30 percent more likely to have heart disease—70 percent more likely if they had experienced emotional abuse as a child—than those with an ACE score of zero.

As for statistics related to early death: The largest group of people with ACE scores of zero who went in for check-ups with their doctors was those over age sixty-five; the next largest, fifty to sixty-five; then thirty-five to forty-nine; and the smallest, nineteen to thirty-four. This breakdown is understandable, because the older you get, the more concerned you become about your health.

However, for those with an ACE score of 2, the size of the age groups was suddenly reversed, indicating this group was suffering a more rapid death toll than those with a score of zero. Those with a score of 4 were not only also reversed, but the initially most common group—those over sixty-five—had almost disappeared. Tragically, the higher your ACE score, the less likely you would make it to your next annual check up.

The study also correlated job performance to ACE scores. Again, compared to those with an ACE score of zero, those with a score of 4 were more than twice as likely to be absent on the job as well as to have serious financial problems, and three times more likely to have serious job problems.

"Finding Your Ace Score"

Anda and Felitti devised ten questions for participants to answer as indicative of adverse childhood experience. The following is their test, which gives an individual an "ACE Score."

While you were growing up, during your first 18 years of life:

1. *Did a parent or other adult in the household often or very often … Swear at you, insult you, put you down, or humiliate you?*
   OR:
   Act in a way that made you afraid that you might be physically hurt?
   Yes   No   *If yes enter 1* _____

2. *Did a parent or other adult in the household often or very often … Push, grab, slap, or throw something at you?*
   OR:
   Ever hit you so hard that you had marks or were injured?
   Yes   No   *If yes enter 1* _____

3. *Did an adult or person at least 5 years older than you ever… Touch or fondle you or have you touch their body in a sexual way?*
   OR:
   Attempt or actually have oral, anal, or vaginal intercourse with you?
   Yes   No   *If yes enter 1* _____

4. *Did you often or very often feel that … No one in your family loved you or thought you were important or special?*
   OR:
   Your family didn't look out for each other, feel close to each other, or support each other?
   Yes   No   *If yes enter 1* _____

5. Did you often or very often feel that ... You didn't have enough to eat, had to wear dirty clothes, and had no one to protect you?
   OR:
   Your parents were too drunk or high to take care of you or take you to the doctor if you needed it?
   Yes   No   If yes enter 1 _____

6. Were your parents ever separated or divorced?
   Yes   No   If yes enter 1 _____

7. Was your mother or stepmother ... Often or very often pushed, grabbed, slapped, or had something thrown at her?
   OR:
   Sometimes, often, or very often kicked, bitten, hit with a fist, or hit with something hard?
   OR:
   Ever repeatedly hit at least a few minutes or threatened with a gun or knife?
   Yes   No   If yes enter 1 _____

8. Did you live with anyone who was a problem drinker or alcoholic or who used street drugs?
   Yes   No   If yes enter 1 _____

9. Was a household member depressed or mentally ill,
   OR:
   Did a household member attempt suicide?
   Yes   No   If yes enter 1 _____

10. Did a household member go to prison?
    Yes   No   If yes enter 1 _____

Now add up your "Yes" answers: _____ **This is your "ACE Score."**

Here is an ACE Study summary sanctioned by the U.S. Department of Health and Human Services:

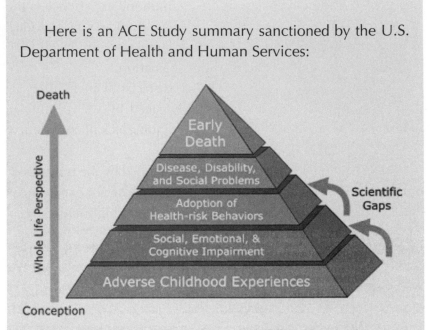

ACE Study - Pyramid - Adverse Childhood Experiences

(Note: the "scientific gap" arrows indicate the influences that move the health and welfare consequences of ACES up the pyramid, in hopes it will be useful in the development of more effective prevention programs.)

The troubling ACE findings have not been refuted. They reveal a very disturbing reality: many of us are using substances like drugs, alcohol, tobacco, and food to escape our childhood pain. In 2008, I gave the ACE test to sixty-five inner city Hyde School 11th graders. No one had a score of zero.

Clearly, we are not born with ACEs. Adverse childhood experiences are learned, and whatever is learned can be unlearned—with treatment. Yet, the medical profession and medical insurance cartel continue to ignore the ACE Study, and thus blindly fail to serve us in this most critical health and welfare issue.

The ACE Study confirms adverse childhood experience is the biggest contributor to the tragic ordeals our society faces today. If we are truly committed to human progress, we are faced with needing a revolutionary societal transformation.

The ACE Study tracked only the worst stuff in families. It doesn't show how we as kids were damaged by such things as parental anger, anxiety, imposed expectations, lack of confidence, lack of commitment, and so on.

Sigmund Freud said we are forever changed by the traumas of our youth. The ACE researchers arbitrarily chose ten experiences for the study; we know there are many other childhood experiences that are also traumatic.

What we should take away from the ACE Study is the long-term consequences of how negative childhood experiences affect us and our children.

Hoffman Institute Helps Adults Address ACEs

The Hoffman Institute is headquartered in the U.S.A. and has organizations in twelve countries. Hoffman has received international fame for its work with personal growth, and particularly for helping individuals with their adverse childhood experiences.

Recognizing that children seek their parents' love from birth by imitating them, these negative experiences make up what Hoffman refers to as a "Negative Love Syndrome." Since this imitation process happens in every generation, Negative Love is the intergenerational pain that is passed down from generation to generation. Everyone is guilty of it, *but no one is to blame for it.* It happened to us when we were children, and we, unknowingly, passed it on.

Bob Hoffman, the founder of the Hoffman Institute, describes the Negative Love Syndrome:

*Created by childhood programming, we acted out these nega-
tivities, over and over again. The pain, the feeling of being
unlovable, and the conflict caused by these negative attitudes,
feelings and behaviors result in personal sufferings and injustices that affect each of us every day.*

How did this Negative Love Syndrome get started in our own lives?

John Bowlby believed infants were born with an "instinctual
behavioral bond" with their mothers that produced stress when
the mother was absent, as well as a drive for the two of them to
seek each other if the child was in fear or pain. Thus, mothers
shape their children with some emotional attributes they will possess and rely upon, both positively and negatively, for the rest of
their lives.

When we as children experienced our parents love being cut
off in some way—such as depression, anger, abandonment, death,
their love becoming conditional—the parental bond was broken
for us and we felt unlovable. This feeling contributed to our inability to relate to ourselves and others with love.

We need to remember that from birth, we are seeking our parents' love to feel secure, so if we feel unlovable, we feel insecure.

> **Parents are an integral part
> of the ego development of
> the child.**

Our taking every-
thing personally as
children may only
add to those feel-
ings, and drive us
to seek our parents'
love even more.

Parents are an integral part of the ego development of the child.
The reason children have such difficulty recognizing or acknowl-
edging inadequacies and faults of their parents is because their
egos are bonded to their parents and such recognitions would
evoke unbearable anxiety within themselves. Many children who
experience physical abuse from a parent may believe they deserve

it; those who experience sexual abuse may repress the memory, because, otherwise, their inner world would fall apart.

These are extremes. But as good and loving as our parents might have been, they were imperfect, and in our process of imitating them to get their love, we imitated their imperfections along with all their good qualities.

If we truly are committed to raise children to become all they were meant to be, then we must make an earnest effort to address the imperfections we internalized from our parents, so we can help our children begin to transcend them in their lives.

We must make an earnest effort to address the imperfections we internalized from our parents.

Our ancestors struggled in their lives, which inevitably created some imperfections in them. These were ultimately internalized in some form by our grandparents, then in our parents, then in us, and then in our children.

We see in this sequence the wisdom of "the apple doesn't fall far from the tree" and "like father, like son;" we see a sex abuser who may have been sexually abused in childhood; we see alcoholism and its affects that continue in families; schizophrenia that has been traced in generations for more than three-hundred years; depression that is passed on; and so on.

Most of us come to recognize this sequencing in life. We set out determined not to have some quality of our parent, and then realize we are repeating it. Or we may see the qualities of our parents determining whom we choose to marry, which can blind us to our natural capacity to love.

There are many kinds of adverse conditions in childhood that can have long-term effects upon one's life: insensitivity to the child's true needs, lack of guidance, domination, disparaging attitudes, erratic behaviors, too much or too little admiration, too much or too few responsibilities, overprotection, having to take sides in parental disagreements, injustices, an angry or emotionless household, and many others.

We are imperfect people, but in striving for excellence we find the excitement of bettering ourselves.

In our childhood, a vital part of ourselves and our ego is shaped by imitating our parents, a process over which we have no control. While much of the ego is a great strength in our lives thanks to the strengths of our parents, there are pockets that represent their imperfections that we imitated.

If we are able to identify those imperfections and then address them, not only will we be able to become a significantly better person in our own life, we will be able to help our children transcend these imperfections in theirs.

> **We are imperfect people, but in striving for excellence we find the excitement of bettering ourselves.**

I have helped thousands of families with this transformative process, and most of them would say the experience changed their lives. I went through it myself and it changed my life.

Recognizing adverse experiences as something that happens to all of us, including our parents, we can see no one is to blame. The great thing is that these negative patterns were learned, and can be unlearned. Of course, we must realize that the process of transcending them will not be easy. But in the end, it will not only improve ourselves, but our children as well.

This is a powerful motivation. We are willing to do things for our kids that we are not willing to do for ourselves. The next two chapters will help us with this task.

Chapter 5

Building Bonds and Mentorships

In this chapter, we will look at how to strengthen nature's parent-child bond, in order to clearly establish ourselves as our children's mentor.

We begin with three initiatives to help us fulfill our responsibility to help our children realize their best and assume self-sufficiency by age nineteen:

1. Ensuring our children emerge from childhood with confidence and enthusiasm, not allowing outside influences to interfere.
2. Inspiring our children by example with high expectations, and helping them reach for those expectations by encouraging and accepting nothing less than their best efforts..
3. Establishing principles of family values, character, and purpose that are distinct from today's achievement culture.

We will also need to address the negative emotional dispositions (NEDs) of our childhood, to free both our children and ourselves of the "Negative Love Syndrome." (To be discussed.)

We know children are naturally curious, so our job is to encourage that curiosity and guide it in productive directions. We need to be open to new areas our kids may seek to explore, but at the same time, challenge them to experience areas of value that we choose—chores, intellectual games at the dinner table, artistic or cultural experiences, etc.

The Power of Imagination

A vital period of children's growth is when they develop their imagination—why Walt Disney's work has become such an integral part of our lives. As another example, when I ask an audience about the 1939 movie *The Wizard of Oz*, the question isn't if they have seen it; but how many times they've seen it. Disney and *Oz* have inspired the imagination of generations.

Imagination is a powerful force in developing a creative mind. Imagination—at any age—opens us to hopes and dreams, which provide the groundwork for the high expectations and vision that we need to fully challenge and draw out our unique potential.

If we are able to firmly hold on to these high expectations and vision, we can establish a productive tension between our vision and our present reality, like holding on to two ends of a stretched rubber band. By continuing to firmly hold on to the vision end of the rubber band, the tension in the rubber band will slowly help bring the reality end to our vision.

Here is a great story about fifteen-year-old Catherine West, a counselor at a summer camp who was asked by the camp director to teach the sailing program. She protested, "But I've never even sailed before!" The director simply said, "Well Catherine, if you don't do it, we just won't have a sailing program this summer."

So Catherine dove in, and at the end of the summer, amazingly saw her group win a sailing regatta. Today she is the "go to" person in a large corporation, where her help is often sought with difficult problems—"Let's see what Catherine thinks."

Catherine says whenever she feels down or stumped, she gets bolstered by reminding herself, "I'm the one who won the regatta." Catherine is an excellent example of an individual who has become comfortable with the tension between high expectations and reality.

But we all know that having high expectations for ourselves and sticking to them is difficult, so difficult that we resist developing challenging visions. I realize today that I had resisted the vision that ultimately led to my 1962 New Year's Eve commitment to change American education. I needed help back then to reach for it—just like our children need our encouragement in developing challenging visions for themselves.

I got that help in 1961 from Sumner Hawley, a colleague and close friend who asked me to play the stage manager in Thornton Wilder's *Our Town*. The part is a visionary who guides the play for the audience. Sumner and I fought over the part almost line by line, because I thought his interpretation stuck me back into the meat-and-potatoes football coach image I believed people had of me.

> **Our children need our encouragement in developing challenging visions for themselves.**

We had the same experience the next year when he cast me in a similar role in Arthur Miller's *All My Sons*.

In essence, I eventually realized I had approached both parts looking for sympathy for the struggles of the characters, while Sumner rightfully wanted me to portray them for the visionary, purposeful, and strong individuals they were.

In acting, I found to truly do justice to the play, you must try to enter the heart and soul of the character you are playing.

Sumner helped me do this. In the process, I was forced to more deeply enter my own heart and soul as a teacher, and my crisis of conscience was ultimately the result. So I have to thank Sumner for seeing and drawing out that visionary potential in me.

Similarly, we want to enhance the deeper development of the heart and soul of our children. We can't force this development in

We want to enhance the deeper development of the heart and soul of our children.

our children, but we can be very sensitive to it and see the opportunities where we can encourage and appreciate it. This desire, attitude, and effort in us are bound to have a deep affect upon our children's growth, since they are seeking our love and approval.

Children's Inner World

It is vitally important that we as parents respect the need of our children to develop their own inner world of thinking; we need to find ways to encourage them to do so. Imagination begins their capability to think creatively, or "outside the box." It provides the foundation for children to ultimately have faith in their hopes and dreams in life.

Consequently, we should be very concerned with today's increasing and overwhelming focus on academic proficiency and test scores in our schools. The emphasis on academic competition has narrowed our children's thinking to more of their left-brain analytical side, thus providing fewer opportunities to express their more creative right-brain intuitive capabilities.

Play, a particularly creative activity for our children, has been a casualty in today's emphasis on academic achievement. The heavy emphasis upon achievement today, not just in school, but overall in child development, has not only put a damper upon child creativity, but upon the vision of our children.

True exploration inevitably involves mistakes and failure, which are valuable because we learn much from them. But in our achievement culture, mistakes and failure are rarely an acceptable option, which encourages us to avoid risks—an attitude that lowers expectations. But when we are raised to high expectations, then we and our children internalize those expectations, no matter how much the achievement culture encourages us to lower them to limit mistakes and failures.

To see this in action, imagine two brand-new high jumpers, with the first setting the bar at four feet, and then the second at six. We know the second jumper is more likely to demonstrate attitude and behavior problems— stomping around in anger, making excuses, being more difficult to coach, etc. But he is also more likely to become the higher jumper—assuming he doesn't quit.

We need to recognize that the high expectations of our families create a high level of tension for our children, which may bring out

> **In our achievement culture, mistakes and failure are rarely an acceptable option, which encourages us to avoid risks.**

attitude and behavior problems in them that reflect in some way the negative patterns we parents internalized in our childhood.

Parent Focus on Effort Over Achievement

We can greatly help our children deal with the tension between high expectations and reality by keeping our focus on our children's best efforts, not on their achievements or failures. A focus on their best encourages them to accept the tension that may involve failure as healthy; a focus on achievements drives them to release the tension for fear of failure, either by letting go of the expectation end of the rubber band or the reality end by living a life based on fantasy, exaggeration, or lies.

While our children seek to imitate us, we also need to realize they simply cannot identify with our achievements as adults. Remember Malcolm's words after I had lost the Florida headmaster position because of my stand on integration:

> *I liked being the son of the head coach, teacher, administrator, but that image had a hollow ring. It was his losing the Florida job that gave me something I could really understand, look up to, and follow.*

At age 10, Malcolm knew how badly I wanted the Florida headmaster position. Then he sees me put an even higher priority on living up to a principle—the school must integrate before I will take the job. He is excited, because he now knows deep in his heart that the high expectations of his family are within his grasp—his doing the right thing and his best will always be more important than what he actually achieves in life.

So as parents, we must take a deeper look at our values than just telling our children what our values are. Since our children read our hearts, we need to learn to see our priorities in life through their eyes.

We can best do that by objectively and dispassionately reviewing our actions and decisions, not our words. This reveals what our kids feel expresses our true expectations of them.

For example, many entering Hyde parents don't realize their kids believe their parents' highest priorities and values relate to good grades and their getting into a good college. Why? Because they see their parents being most interested in those aspects of their lives.

This is an unrecognized dilemma of many American families today. Many parents assume they are focused on developing character, when actually their kids see their parents placing a higher priority on the values of our achievement culture.

An obvious example of this is cheating. Annual polls have told us for over thirty years that the vast majority of American students

> **We can best do that by objectively and dispassionately reviewing our actions and decisions, not our words.**

cheat. The fact that parents have paid little attention to this reality while increasing their concern over academic achievement is a clear statement to their kids of what they value, whether parents realize it or not.

This paradox in American values was recently highlighted in an online survey of 3,600 students conducted by The School for Ethical Education. The survey found 95 percent of the students admitted to cheating in the past year, while 57 percent agreed or strongly agreed with the statement, "It is morally wrong to cheat." My interpretation is that American children hear our words saying cheating is morally wrong, but they know our larger concern is their academic achievement. Kids listen to our hearts, not our words.

I think most American parents believe character is their top priority in raising their kids. I think they would honestly be shocked to realize how much our achievement culture, combined with parental focus on their kids' achievement as the primary means to succeed in life, has led American kids to put less and less value upon their character.

After the AT&T breakup over 20 years ago, I was asked by the CEO of one of its companies to meet with his leadership staff. They knew they would have to learn how to compete like other corporations, and thus needed to think more like entrepreneurs and not just a monopoly that negotiated with the government to set telephone rates.

Eye-Opening Parenting Program

In 1998, after twenty-four years of working with teenagers and parents in school settings, Laura and Malcolm Gauld wrote a parenting book, *The Biggest Job We'll Ever Have (Scribner 2002)*, and developed the Biggest Job® program to help parents across the country address the problem of having their emphasis on character in the home overwhelmed by the achievement culture in schools and society. As the dying professor Morrie says to his pupil Mitch in the best-selling book *Tuesdays with Morrie* by Mitch Albom:

"Our culture values the wrong things and you have to be strong enough to say that if the culture is not working, don't buy into it."

The Biggest Job program begins by asking parents to visualize their kids twenty years from now, and to consider:

- What principles do you hope they will honor?
- What qualities do you want them to possess?
- What kind of people do you hope they will become?

Program participants make a list; we find the lists are similar, regardless of geography or demographics. The lists invariably include items such as: Respect for others; be happy; be fulfilled; character; employed; honesty; courage; resourceful; integrity; confidence; leadership; peace of mind; humility; willingness to take risks; communicator; trusting; self-esteem; parenthood; to be excited about life; loving people; socially active; responsible.

As all of us think about the items on the list, we realize how central character is to what we really want for our children's lives.

Then this program has an exercise where we ask the audience to call out those qualities by which we are evaluated in today's culture. We deliberately do not give any further explanations, and again, regardless of geography or demographics, here are some of the answers we consistently receive: salary; job title; education; your house; your neighborhood; your car; where you vacation; how your children are doing; where they go to school; appearance; clothes; weight; how you speak; birthday parties.

We ask participants, "Suppose you were living in a character culture. How would we be perceived?"

Here are qualities that seem to appear on every list: attitude; effort; service to others; community service; integrity; courage; role model; faith; passion; perseverance; humor; dreams.

Then we put these lists side by side and ask, "What do they say to you? Think about how we operate in our daily lives with these very different paradigms."

Clearly the character culture and achievement culture are at odds. As parents think back to the lists of what they really want for their kids, they see it matches up to the character culture, not the achievement culture.

A telling comment came from a participating father from San Francisco:

"Although I tell my kids that the most important things in life are those qualities listed on the right hand side of the page [the character culture], I have to admit I live most of my life on the left hand side of the page. I guess I show my kids that achievement is more important. After all, that is where I spend most of my time and effort."

I admire this parent's commitment to his kids. It is this kind of sensitivity that enables us to realize nature's powerful parent-child bond.

As I sat at the table with six executives and the CEO, a key question I asked the director of personnel was, "If you had to choose between one team who had expertise but not character and another team who had character but not expertise, who would you choose?" After long thought, he chose the expertise, saying he'd work on the character. I looked over at the CEO to acknowledge the leadership problem he had. Expertise is something we learn; character is developed over a lifetime.

I had expected that answer, because for over fifty years, our educational system has increasingly emphasized academic achievement at the expense of character development. I personally think our recent economic breakdown can primarily be traced to a lack of character: greed.

To create nature's parent-child bond, there is a commitment we parents must make, a commitment to the child's future. It happens almost naturally for birthing mothers, who have a unique nine-month experience developing the infant, culminating in the difficult but amazing creation of the child.

What Kind of Parent Am I?

At the child's birth, mothers have already established a bond; they must find a way to continue that commitment. But fathers and adopting parents begin without that bond and therefore must develop a meaningful commitment in order to achieve it.

I'm amused remembering my thoughts the first day my first child Malcolm was born. Looking back, I realize the problems that *that* father would have had developing a bond with Malcolm, Laurie and Gigi, once they became teenagers.

It is 1954; I'm a teacher-coach at a boy's prep school looking in at my newborn son in his hospital basinet, imagining him accomplishing all the things in athletics and school I hadn't accomplished. Needless to say, I was not on the path to developing a parent-child bond.

Being in a boys school, I had a hidden preference for boys—at least I thought it was hidden. When Laurie was born, my thought was well, yes, we ought to have a girl. But then when the nurse announced to me our third child was also a girl, the look on my face moved her to flip up the blanket to prove the evidence, and the first words my wife said to me after Gigi's birth were, "I'm so sorry." Blanche apparently read my heart better than I had.

I knew from my own upbringing that the growth of our kids needed to come first in our lives. Fortunately I had married an exceptional mother, so I could depend on Blanche to make sure I was doing what I needed to do as a father, while I intensely pursued my career and ultimately my commitment to change American education.

I felt I was being a good father. But one day as I watched Mal and Laurie playing (Gigi was not yet born,) I asked myself, do I love these things? As I explored this question, I had a terrible feeling that in a catastrophe, I might save myself, not them. I would ultimately learn from a future experience that I would in fact save them, but at that time I was still in the process of developing a commitment that would cement my parent-child bond, and would include confronting my male bias.

This is the difficulty we have as parents: we have no problem holding our kids to their best, but who holds us as parents to our best? No matter how good we are as parents, we are imperfect people. We point out the imperfections in our kids and expect them to deal with them. But what is the process by which we recognize our own imperfections and then deal with them? Who points them out to us?

We were somewhat fortunate in raising our children by principles—remember the story of me getting frustrated when I couldn't find two socks that matched, and three-year-old Malcolm saying, "If you act that way about it, you won't get any!" Several

What is the process by which we recognize our own imperfections and then deal with them?

more times in life, where my temper got the best of me, my kids just laughed, and I ended up just feeling foolish—because that's what I did to them when they got really mad.

Hyde Process of Self Discovery

Hyde parents have the advantage of a community that helps them look at themselves, their attitudes and dispositions. Using Hyde's five words – Curiosity, Courage, Concern, Leadership, Integrity – Hyde parents go through the same self-discovery process as the students and teachers; in character development, parents are the primary teachers and the home the primary classroom.

The process enables us as parents to reestablish character as the source of the primary values in our families. We also utilize the five Hyde principles:

Destiny: Each of us is gifted with a unique potential that defines a destiny.

Humility: We believe in a power and a purpose beyond ourselves.

Conscience: We attain our best through character and conscience.

Truth: Truth is our primary guide.

Brother's Keeper: We help each other achieve our best.

The principles give us a foundation on which to build our family relationships:

- Destiny reminds us to respect each other.
- Humility provides a good check on our egos.
- Conscience helps bring out our best selves.
- Truth over harmony maintains trust within the family.
- Brother's Keeper keeps our family relationships strong and each of us at our best.

This works for Hyde families. But my larger point is that parents everywhere can firmly establish the values and principles their families stand for, and then clearly demonstrate to their children that these values and principles have the highest priority in their lives, regardless of the values of the achievement culture.

So at this point, let us assume we become very sensitive to our kids' development, doing things like encouraging their imagination when they are young, being able to keep our focus on their character in our achievement culture, and learning how to effectively support our part of nature's parent-child bond.

Now we are ready for the deepest part—how do we deal with the dispositions of our parenting and ourselves over which we have the least control, that is, the negative patterns we internalized in childhood from how we ourselves were parented?

This is also the hardest part, because we have to get really honest about our childhood, which means including revisiting events we either found painful, or chose to forget, regarding our parents.

Chapter 6

Completing Bonds and Mentorships

In this chapter, we look at the importance of addressing the negative emotional dispositions (NEDs) of our childhood, to free both our children and ourselves of the negative love syndrome.

This is very difficult work for us, because it requires us to remember some painful experiences, and it is quite natural to forget that which is painful. The part of our brain (hippocampus) that is responsible for memory can literally "forget" or suppress some unpleasant events we lived through, particularly those in childhood, while another part of our brain (amygdala) will always "remember" how we felt about it and then coped with it.

For example, I have a fear of heights; I have stayed away from open balconies as long as I can remember. My mother said I rolled off the bed twice when I was a baby. I suspect that may be the cause, assuming it wasn't an inborn fear, or from another experience I have since forgotten.

Similarly, we have negative patterns—attitudes, behaviors, moods, biases—that we express in life. We may develop excuses for them, but we may really have no idea where they originated.

If we weren't born with them, we must have learned them in our process of imitating our parents.

Negative Patterns Passed On Through Generations

Since we love and look up to our parents, there is going to be a strong tendency to forget negative patterns we internalized from them, because it is painful to make that connection. With some exceptions, I find that parents have great difficulty making an objective and honest evaluation of their parents' negative patterns.

We may feel compassion and be supportive of such parents, feeling they are just being respectful. While that is an understandable response from us, we would be doing these parents and their children a great disservice to not move beyond that response.

This is not about their parents' parenting; it's about the negative patterns that have been passed down from each generation, which like a virus, keep both ourselves and our children from doing our best, and from fully realizing our spirit, unique potential, and natural capacity to love in life.

> **We need to address what our parents didn't do for us.**

If we do not honestly identify these negative patterns, then our heads and our egos will continue to live in one world, while our hearts and souls inhabit a deeper truth.

We cannot be living a meaningful and fulfilling life if our outer self does not fully reflect our inner self. And our children will follow our example.

This means we need to address what our parents didn't do for us, a vitally important area of our childhood that we now need to repair or transform, not just for our sake, but for our children as well.

To undergo this important transformation, we will need to let go of our parents, so we can accept that our efforts are not meant to criticize them. We must always remember our parents could not help us with these areas, because when they were children, their parents did not help them with these areas. It will be very difficult for us to deal with these areas if we attach blame to them.

When it comes to negative childhood experience in the home, we all have them, but no one is to blame for them.

We need to remember, when it comes to negative childhood experience in the home, we all have them, but no one is to blame for them. If we maintain this attitude, we will focus on changing for the better, and not get stuck in the negatives of the past.

Anything that may connect or even imply fault with our parents is difficult for us to address. As a child, our parents were an integral part of our ego, so to find fault with them is to find deep fault within ourselves as children, which is not fair and must be resisted.

However, I do find a few parents bitterly criticizing their parents, emphasizing the negatives while remembering few positives. I believe this is their way of living with the problems and disappointments they are enduring in life—in essence their parents failed to give them the proper foundation in life, or in more scientific terms, failed to support their ego development in those earlier years. So they survive by blaming their parents, subconsciously saying, "If you knew how really bad I was parented, you'd know how really well I'm doing."

It simply is very difficult for us to objectively evaluate our parents' parenting. To do it effectively, we must be able to see them as individuals beyond ourselves.

Understanding Parents as Individual People

I certainly sought my mother's love; she told me that when she got cross with me when I was very little, I'd crawl under the bed until she said it was all right to come out. But the trust I had in her led me through her divorce, a strained relationship with my step-father and her alcoholism. As I grew into a teenager, I always trusted our bond, and came to understand her alcoholism as her problem, not related to me. Then as her insanity took hold, I was in a position to provide some guidance to my parents. Understanding them as people helped me in this new role.

I thank my parents, and particularly my stepfather, for preparing me for self-sufficiency. It gave me the ability to begin to evaluate how I was parented, something I find many parents fail to do effectively, because of their inability to let go of their parents.

If we haven't fully let go of our parents, we are not fully head of our house, and our children know it.

We parents need to let go of our child at the end of adolescence. But more emphasis needs to be put on us letting go of our parents. Once we start having children, we must become head of our house—no exceptions. If we haven't fully let go of our parents, we are not fully head of our house, and our children know it.

Of course as adults we want to listen to and respect our parents. But if our mind or emotions are still tied up in what our parents are thinking or feeling, then we haven't let go of our parents. If we can't honestly go back and remember how our childhood really was and objectively evaluate how our parents raised us, both the good and the bad, then we are doing our children—and even our parents—a great disservice.

Thanks to our parents, the vast majority of us internalized a foundation of positive childhood experiences in our home, which creates within us what I call positive emotional dispositions (PEDs.) These PEDs represent qualities—moral character, values, attitudes, sense of purpose, demeanor, etc.—that form our foundation for a meaningful life.

However our parents were imperfect people, so we also internalized an area of negative childhood experiences in our home, which created within us what I call negative emotional disposi-

> **This *Negative Love Syndrome* leads us to express love through the negative patterns we experienced in childhood, not through our natural capacity to love.**

tions (NEDs.) These NEDs represent negative patterns within us—attitudes, behaviors, moods, biases, etc.—that keep us from fully realizing our unique potential and true best in life.

The problem of these NEDs within us is that they not only lead us to negative attitudes and behaviors, they also block us from fully expressing our unique potential and spirit.

This *Negative Love Syndrome* leads us to express love through the negative patterns we experienced in childhood, not through our natural capacity to love. If we don't address the NEDs, they will cause problems to our bond.

Examples of Negative Emotional Dispositions

Let me use some examples:

Say our parent was critical. In order to get our parent's love, we imitated our parent and became critical. But our friends didn't like it; we didn't like ourselves, and we resented our parent for making us critical. But that is what we learned love is—why it's called the Negative Love Syndrome. We internalize the critical quality as love and it becomes a NED in us.

When we grow up we may choose a mate who is critical because that is what we learned love is. Or maybe we rebel and decide to become non-judgmental, or marry someone who is. But in either case, we are reacting to a negative pattern with another pattern, not with our own natural capacity to love. And in either case, the pattern is not our own and therefore will create a difficulty with our bond with our children.

Anger can be a big NED. It is an intense emotion, and so as children we internalize it from our parent; it can easily become a substitute expression for love (eg: think of families we know that are quick to angry fights and reconciliations.) Or, one parent could have anger problems and the other may be non-responsive, so the child imitates two different models or patterns: anger and being non-responsive. In the same family, one child may grow up to be an angry person who marries someone who is non responsive, while another child becomes non-responsive while marrying an angry person.

As these children go on to form their own families, we see these patterns continue. In all of this, anger is playing a major role in defining who we are, and how we love. But remember, anger is not part of our unique potential, or our natural capacity to love. It is simply a NED we internalized in childhood and carried into life.

Clearly, the solution is to treat the anger like a virus. If it's in the parent, then through the imitation process, it will also be in the child. Step One: Get parent and child both to acknowledge they have the anger virus. Since it was learned in childhood, it can be unlearned. Step Two: Get them to work together to help each other get rid of the virus. Synergy can be a powerful medicine, especially when it involves family members.

Addressing My Negative Patterns

I went to the Hoffman Institute at age 80 because I felt it could help me become a better person. I have always expressed anger, but I chalked it up to my intensity in getting the best out of myself and others.

Hoffman starts you out with your childhood name—mine was Joey. With their deep process, they helped me realize that my anger, frustration, impatience, sarcasm, and "my way or the highway" attitudes were often actually tied to times when people didn't listen or ignored me, which put me back to being the impotent little Joey I was as a kid who no one took seriously!

I was amazed at this revelation and delighted to realize that these attitudes were not the real me, but simply deep reactions I carried over from my childhood. That was four years ago, and I've had a much happier and productive life after shedding those attitudes. Honestly, they are no longer a part of me.

Both my brother Tom and I internalized the anger NED from our mother, who in turn internalized it from her alcoholic mother. I think my ability to make such a remarkably quick transformation is a combination of my Hyde experience, my age, and expressing my natural self. The reader is exposed to the process I experienced in Chapter 10.

Physical, mental, or emotional abuse without intervention, become NEDs. The parent who is so abused as a child has to believe that s/he deserves the abuse and that the parent is basically doing it out of love, because the alternative is unthinkable—remember, the parent is part of his/her ego.

So if a father's NED leads him to also abuse his child, it's what he has learned about how to love his child. However, should the father choose to rebel, he might do so by either shunning physical contact or by expressing excessive affection with his child. But in all cases, he is treating the child based on the child as himself growing up,

> **He is treating the child based on the child as himself growing up.**

and the parent-child bond is lost. The child wants to be treated as a unique individual, not like he was his father when he was a child.

Say the mother, because of her own childhood experience, seeks to control the household and the children, while the father takes a more submissive role. While her NED may not seem to cause problems for children when they are young, once they become adolescents they will be increasingly caught between wanting to please the controlling parent vs. rebelling in an attempt to express their developing unique potential.

What Parent Control Means

The depth of the mother's control vs. the spirit of the adolescent may produce many outcomes in life. The adolescent in life may also become a "controller," or imitate the father in becoming someone who is more submissive, or simply rebel and take on a pattern of someone who fights authority and refuses to obey the rules. (Of course, the father may be the controller, and the mother submissive.) And there are children who stand up for themselves and they and their parents may ultimately struggle through the control problem to find some middle ground.

In dealing with parents, I find that control was often a major concern in their upbringing that ultimately influenced how they decided to raise their own children. In many cases they also sought to control their children because that is what they had internalized as love. In other cases they rebelled, and went overboard in letting their children express themselves. In either case, the unique parent-child bond was inevitably lost, because, beyond the NEDs involved, the parent

> **The parent is raising the child as s/he was raised, or in opposition to how s/he was raised.**

is raising the child as s/he was raised, or in opposition to how s/he was raised.

If instead, parents internalized and expressed their submissive parent in a controlled household in their parenting, then their children feel that parent didn't give them guidance or a sense of self- worth. And if parents rebelled against the pattern of the submissive parent, then their parenting simply took on problems of the controlling parent.

Roadblocks in Parent-Child Bonding

In a larger sense, the deeper problem here is the interference of one's upbringing in the sacred bonding of parent and child. The bonding must always come first, which then enables parents to draw from their own childhood experience those lessons that really fit well in developing each child.

But moving beyond how we were parented can be very difficult, because the source of our love for our parents was from imitating them.

For an extreme example, when I help a mother deal with sexual abuse as a child by her father, there may be difficulty in even her memory of the abuse because of the deep sense of disloyalty. Then she needs to forgive herself for allowing it to happen, because of her adult sense of responsibility. She must come to realize that as a child she had virtually no choice, because her parent was an integral part of her child's ego. This is particularly true if she didn't feel she could tell her mother what was happening.

Our society must hold the father responsible for his behavior. In reality, the source of his problem is in all probability the attitudes and behaviors he internalized as a child. So if we truly wish to address major problems like sexual abuse and other societal problems outlined in the ACE study, then our society needs to begin to address NEDs in much the same way the Salk vaccine treated Polio. That is, treating NEDs requires a preventive approach that will dramatically improve human lives.

Whether I liked it or not, these deeper feelings existed in me, and affected how I dealt with myself and others.

When I went to the Hoffman Institute—which I consider an excellent extension of the Hyde process—I felt love for my mother and stepfather, but some resentments for my father for not standing up for my sister Joan, who had chosen to live with him following the divorce. In his second marriage, Joan got treated like a second-class citizen.

The Hoffman process took me to a deeper level within myself where I realized I was in denial that my father had abandoned me in life, but that my mother and my stepfather at times had abandoned me as well. Whether I liked it or not, these deeper feelings existed in me, and affected how I dealt with myself and others.

The process also helped me experience real compassion for the NEDs all three of my parents experienced in their childhoods, which helped me understand that their failures where I was concerned were a consequence of their NEDs, not flaws in them as people. I ended up with a deeper love and appreciation for my parents and a warm empathy for my father.

What Hoffman helped me do is separate some very deep feelings of abandonment within myself from my parents so I could fully deal with those feelings and get rid of them as one would shed a virus.

It reaffirmed for me once again what a better world we would have if we would help each other address our childhood NEDs.

We now see what the roadblocks are to a close and powerful mentoring parent-child bond.

To deepen those bonds, we have to ask ourselves, how deeply are we dealing with life? Is our heart and soul dominating our head and ego? Is our spirit being fully expressed in our life? If not, we can be pretty sure negative and unresolved childhood experiences are upsetting our heart and soul, whether our head realizes it or not.

Once we can identify the NEDs that resulted from negative patterns we experienced in childhood, we can explain to our children what we are doing, and ask them to also identify their negative patterns, so we could compare our lists with them (A list of negative patterns is provided in Chapter 10.)

After comparing these lists, some common ground is reached. Then parents and kids can synergistically begin to work together to transcend these viruses.

Chapter 7

Examples of Establishing Bonds

To review:

- Our ability 1) To challenge and draw out our children's best, and 2) To develop their self-sufficiency by age nineteen, establishes the foundation for our parent-child bond and our role as their mentors.

- These bonds are forged by gradually giving our children new responsibilities, continually expecting their best, while never allowing them to quit on themselves. This more challenging relationship leads our children to begin to trust us as a mentor.

- We recognize our children seek our love and thus we do not seek their love, instead we only seek our children's best, which reassures our children of our deeper devotion and love. We ask for nothing else from our children.

- We enhance both our bond and our mentorship by being sensitive to our children's natural development. We look for ways to support our children's natural curiosity to explore, particularly encouraging our children's imagination and creativity.

- We recognize our bond and mentorship can be threatened and even broken by the negative emotional dispositions (NEDs) we internalized in our childhood, which recreate in our families the Negative Love Syndrome we experienced growing up.

The tragedy in American childrearing today is that NEDs compromise or break parent-child bonds, leading to failed mentorship, with children often going off-track.

To some degree, we all internalize NEDs and a Negative Love Syndrome in our childhood.

Two years ago I asked four Hyde teachers if they would share their family stories since they all had gone through the Hoffman process. As I was writing this book, I realized their stories would be a good starting point to understand all family stories. I later asked for responses from their husbands and adult children. I have changed names to keep the families anonymous

These family stories illustrate ways in which NEDs influence lives, and how it is never too late to secure and solidify the parent-child bond and the mentoring role of parents.

The Murphy Family

The Murphys represented a solid American family. They attended church regularly, believed in good character, were active members of the community, and chose schools that would prepare their four children to attend good colleges.

Mom writes about her upbringing:

I grew up in a family with six children. As the oldest girl, my role was to help take care of the younger ones. My mother, a self-professed perfectionist, had her "hands full" and was often

"beside herself." When she was upset, it was hard on all of us. She had migraines and over-worked herself to exhaustion. She would then lose her temper and begin yelling and making threats. I remember crying and desperately wishing I could be a better kid so she could be happy.

Mom's goals seemed to be to keep us looking good (clean, well-dressed, behaving well,) clean the house until it was "spotless," and make a quality home, with cooked meals every night. This translated into many problems—we fought, got dirty, ruined clothes, messed up the house, and complained about whatever we had for dinner. Rarely were these events taken in stride. Instead we were made to feel we were ruining our family with our misbehavior. In addition, I heard a lot from my father about how cute and precious my little sisters were. I got the message that if I did a better job in making sure they were taken care of, life could be better for me—Mom might be happy, and Dad might think I was as special as my sisters.

All of this was a recipe for helping to create me as a perfectionist, image-conscious, and controlling parent. I tried not to repeat my mother's mistakes—the house did not have to be spotless (but don't track in mud!) The kids did not have to look perfect (but they better not get TOO dirty) I had a lot more patience than Mom did (usually.) To top it off, my oldest son was a premature baby who suffered from asthma as well as ADHD. I wanted him to do well in school (bad grades were not an option if you are a really good mother.) So I spent a lot of time drilling him, working with him, making things work for him. I tried to help him feel good about himself by putting things into place so he could be successful.

This was a lot of work—in fact, exhausting. I had little energy left for the rest of my children, my husband or me. Then, imagine my dismay, at age seventeen my son fell apart. In my most important job—which I believed was raising a successful *and happy child—I had failed miserably. He was dishonest, lazy, self-destructive, and filled with self-doubts, as well as being rude and ungrateful.*

After a terrible year, we found Hyde School. The first thing I was horrified to learn was my best intentions were in part responsible for my child's problems. I had sent the message to him that said: You need your mom to set things up for you. You are not capable of figuring things out on your own. In fact, you are incapable of any success unless Mom paves the way first.

Secondly, we had little trust between us. This was in part because I had never shared my own struggles with him. I thought I was protecting him—he didn't need to know I did stupid things in high school—that I was unsure of myself—that I had feelings of self- doubt.

So he saw me as someone who had it all together. He couldn't tell me about his problems and fears because he knew I wouldn't understand—I had never felt that way or acted that way. I acted so self-assured, knew all the answers, and never seemed to have any doubts. How could he trust me? There was no way he thought I could relate to him or his feelings.

The Hyde process taught me that I needed to work on myself to inspire my kid. This didn't mean to fix all my flaws and be perfect—but instead to show humility, to admit those flaws, struggle openly, and be honest about my feelings. This is what I wanted from my son, so I needed to model it. I also learned that I needed to let go of him—to stop sending him the message that he needed my help in the running of his life. I needed to let him make mistakes and give him the room to figure out what to do. That is what he needed to build his confidence. I had it all wrong! It was not the outcomes and results of his endeavors that would build his self-esteem. Instead, it was the journey of working hard and putting in effort that made him begin to feel good about himself.

*

On this Hyde journey, I needed to look at all those patterns my mother and father had taught me, those patterns that I was teaching my kids. My mom had showed me by her example that I should not feel like I was a great person. Obviously she did not think that way about herself, so how could I? She taught me that the only way to feel good was to be perfect—an impossibility. As a consequence, I rarely felt proud of what I did because I knew it was not perfect. My dad taught me that controlling and bossing others was how you showed that you loved them—and I loved my kids and husband so much. Consequently, I controlled and bossed my entire family.

Also, my mother taught me how important other people's opinions of my family were. If we could look good on the outside, then we could feel like we were a happy and successful family. But I found even when that happened—when my own family was complimented by others—it was a hollow feeling that never really rang true.

Because of the Hyde process, I recognized those patterns and saw them for what they were—destructive and not the "real me." At my core I was a person who was honest and hardworking, one who had a commitment to herself to be the best that she could be. This was not perfectionism, instead it was about overcoming my obstacles, to look at myself and laugh instead of cry, to be the same person on the outside as I was on the inside.

The Hyde process asked me to take risks—to do things I would have never agreed to do if I had not been here! One of those was to complete the high ropes course. As I stood below looking at the thin ropes swaying in the breeze, I realized that this would be one of the toughest physical challenges I had ever faced. Overcoming my self-doubt and fears, I scaled the tree and after sixty minutes of terror and tears, completed the course. I had a different feeling about myself as I rode the zip line at the end. I learned that I could do things that I was afraid to do. I might not look good or succeed, but that was not the point. It was the effort that made me proud, not the outcome. I learned that taking a risk and being vulnerable was what I needed to do to feel proud of myself.

The Hyde seminars asked me to speak from the heart about my true feelings. Being honest with myself and others lifted me up in my own eyes. My son saw from my example of how to do this. I saw that the Hyde process would put him in positions of taking risks—asking him to do things he did not think he could, to talk about those inner feelings. The journey of his effort would reap rewards in how he saw himself—as a strong person who does not quit.

I always wanted to be a strong and courageous parent. During my years in the parent program, I learned that being strong and having courage did not mean looking like superwoman. Instead, being strong meant to have the willingness to show my fears, share my struggles, and to be vulnerable. Having courage did not mean acting unafraid; instead it was being afraid, showing it and doing the scary thing anyway! I learned that the parent I was meant to be was the perfect parent for my kid. It was the woman inside who was not controlled by her parents' patterns of low self-esteem, perfection, and control. Instead it was the woman who parented (and lived her life) through her conscience and convictions, with grit and grace, with love and commitment—the woman who valued her own unique potential as much as she valued her children's. I learned that if I wanted them to go after their destiny, I must show them by going after my own.

The Hyde process gave me my voice, allowed me to hear my conscience and helped me to grow up. As a parent, I now feel confident that I am setting the example for the kind of person I expect my children to be—not perfect, but real. Not always happy, but fulfilled and proud. I believe I am going after my unique potential, living a life worth living—the one I was meant to live. My hope is to inspire my children to live the life they are meant to live as well.

This seems clear from Mom's paper: 1) She learned—particularly from her mother—that a parent's love is expressed by controlling your children's lives, and 2) Since she was not one of the "cute" and favored daughters growing up, she must do something extra in life to gain the love of others.

As we read her story, we see her removing these shackles from her thoughts and feelings and giving more attention, respect, and even love in her efforts to simply improve herself and her parenting.

In essence, she is discarding her parenting based on the NEDs she internalized in her childhood, and in its place, build on her own parent-child bond. After one of her Hyde seminars she wrote:

During his growin-up years I often tried to pave the way for my oldest son. I thought if I worked to "put things in place" for him, he would have success and feel good about himself. However, during a parent meeting, a Hyde faculty member said, "It does not matter what you say, he knows that deep down you really don't believe he can stand on his own two feet."

That hit me like a ton of bricks. She was right. No matter what I said, he could read my heart. I did not have faith in him! I wanted to, but up until that point I had not let myself take that risk. That day I made a conscious decision to truly let go and have faith in him …. It was up to me to truly let go.

This has stuck with me through the years. When he had to leave college for a semester, I did not rescue him, but had faith he would figure it out. He did! As he struggles in his life after college, I listen, but do not try to fix. I believe deep in my heart that he can—and will—figure out whatever challenges life has for him.

Dad writes:

Before I came to Hyde, I had lost my confidence as a parent. I was an active parent, but that wasn't enough for our family. As my kids entered their teen years, it became harder to solve their problems and keep them on task. When confronted with uncertain outcomes, I either backed away or ended up angry ...

Hyde gave me parenting insight that helped me differentiate between what I was doing versus asking myself why I was doing it. I had spent too much energy and time trying to keep or make my oldest son happy. I did this because I thought this is what I was supposed to do. It's what I saw my friends and family do for their kids, yet my kid was very unhappy. He was unhappy with himself and unhappy with me. I was unhappy with him and myself. I was taking responsibility for how he was feeling.

The biggest change in my parenting came when I accepted that failure and struggle were good for my kids. As soon as I accepted that my kids needed to struggle and fail on their own, my parenting instincts made so much more sense for me. "Struggle is good" became an axiom and central tenant to my parenting. With each encounter or interaction with my kids, I now question if there is an opportunity for my kids to struggle, fail, or succeed on their own merit. Do I need to get out of the way?

When I walked away from the responsibility for how my kids felt, they accepted that responsibility. Hyde helped with that transition and I am grateful.

Dad is giving us great insight into parenting. It is not our responsibility to make our kids happy; instead, it is our responsibility to make sure our kids struggle to the point that they sometimes fail as well as succeed. Like a caterpillar whose struggles in the cocoon is developing wings strong enough to fly, so is the child who struggles in childhood developing a character strong enough to fulfill a destiny.

The oldest son, Mike, writes:

Growing up in the Murphy family was an adventure; the family dynamic was constantly changing. As the oldest I was the guinea pig, and it has been said many times since I graduated from Hyde that my parents refined their parenting techniques on me.

One thing about growing up "Murphy" that I'm eternally grateful for is my necessity to share my opinions. We always let one another know how we felt. Rarely was an emotion ever bottled, and I am much better off because of this.

The main conflicts I had with my parents were in my attempts of rebellion. At sixteen, my life changed. I started to drift into cliques and away from my athletic friends because I did not make the soccer team at school. Eventually my new friends and I spent most of our free time altering ourselves. This was very exciting to me.

At home most of our fights started with my parents being concerned about what I was doing when I went out at night or who I was spending time with or what my priorities needed to be. I, of course, rejected everything they said. How could they know what it's like to be a teenage boy (never really occurring to me my father was once a teenager) plus what they wanted me to do with all my time was quite lame.

As the teenage years rolled on, I became more and more out of control and eventually addicted to drugs. Looking back, I see it really wasn't one particular drug, but the event of getting high and altering my perceptions. This was my priority. My parents didn't like this very much; enter major conflict.

Honestly, I still struggle with instant gratification today. I am certainly a lot better today than I was before Hyde, but I think this will be a lifelong struggle. I want what I want when I want it. The marshmallow experiment [see below] is like a broken record inside my brain's ongoing conversation within myself.

Before Hyde I didn't struggle with instant gratification. I always gave into it. Class sucks? Skip it! Parents grounded me? Sneak out! Etc.

During Hyde, instant gratification was something I really started to think about for the first time. I think in part this is because my actions and consequences were laid out so plainly for me to internalize. For instance, before Hyde if I didn't do my homework, I could lie and get away with it or just bullshit my way through lessons and aptitude. At Hyde, this didn't work. I knew that if I skipped doing my homework to play video games in the dorm common room, Miss Maggio would tear me apart the next day in English. So I had to delay.

After Hyde, I went to college. Not a great environment to refine delaying instant gratification, but I was wise enough to survive school. Now where I really learned about my internal discipline was in my life, post-college: the working world. Living on your own sans parents in a city on the other side of the country really snaps you into shape. I was poor coming out of school, so I wised up fast that if I want to pay my rent—I cannot go out drinking every night. I learned that if I wanted to pursue any of my hobbies, financially I had to make sure my bills were paid first. Now after four years since I graduated, I am getting good at restraining myself from every silly whim that comes across my head.

Before Hyde, I saw my parents as perfect. They didn't make mistakes; they didn't fight with one another, and they were never tempted to do the wrong thing. Because of this perception, I saw their expectations as unobtainable and many times never tried to meet those expectations.

The Importance of Delayed Gratification

Why parenting well is so challenging has a lot to do with gratification.

All kids begin as slaves to instant gratification, so our job as parents is to help them learn delayed gratification, the power of which was confirmed in the famous "marshmallow test" at Stanford university in the 1960s:

A group of four-year-olds was given the choice of one marshmallow now or two later if they would wait until the researcher conducting the experiment finished an "errand."

Some of the children grabbed the marshmallows while others were able to wait. Then, those two groups were later observed in high school. The differences were astonishing.

The grabbers tended to have a more troubled psychological portrait, to be stubborn and indecisive, easily upset by frustrations, to think of themselves as unworthy, to be prone to envy, and to overreact to irritations with a sharp temper, provoking arguments and fights.

However the "waiters" were more socially competent, personally effective, self-assertive, and better able to cope with frustrations of life. They embraced challenges, were self-reliant and confident, trustworthy and dependable and took initiative. Their SATs averaged 210 points higher than the other group.

These two groups were observed over forty years and these differences essentially held up. All of this predicted by whether or not a four-year old was trained in delayed gratification!

If you had watched these little four-year-old "waiters" during those seemingly endless ten to fifteen minutes until the researcher returned so they could earn the extra marshmallow, you might better appreciate their character. To sustain themselves in their struggle, they covered their eyes so they wouldn't have to stare at temptation, or rested their heads on their arms, talked to themselves, sang, played games with their hands and feet, even tried to go to sleep.

Those children had parents who had taught them something very important: the second marshmallow was something they wanted, and they were confident their character would get it for them. These families were on a successful parenting track in life, although a challenging one.

But during Hyde, this started to change. One of our first family weekends was actually dedicated to this very topic. I remember my dad crying, telling me "I am not superman" and telling me he loved me no matter who I was, but like many lessons learned at Hyde, you never really understand them until years and years later.

After Hyde, like me, my parents were different people. They weren't dominating personalities with totalitarian rules anymore. They saw the changes I made at school and trusted me for the first time in years.

I see my parents today as advisers with infallible intentions for me. While our relationship is much less intense today, not a day goes by that their voices do not enter my internal conversations. I emulate their behavior more today than ever before, I think in part just because I am no longer a child. I miss them.

We see Mike's mother plays a controlling role because of her childhood NED, and thus may have failed to help him develop his senses of responsibility and of delayed gratification in his early years. However, she and her husband are able to transform their parenting when Mike was seventeen for the benefit of all their children.

Younger brother Paul writes:
Growing up as a child in our family was fun. My father came to all of my sporting events, and used to throw the ball with Bob and me while we would run crossing routes across the yard.

Mike was my role model; I wore his number, I aspired to be like him. I was always Mom's helper; I liked seeing her happy and liked making her life easy because Mike was a handful. I wanted to be the perfect child, who was no stress on anyone. Subsequently, I became shy, and didn't like a lot of interaction. Wow, has that changed since I was a boy.

As I got older, things seemed to unravel at the seams in our family. My older brother was starting to behave out of control, and his attitude was selfish and nasty. I saw my parents for the first time throw their hands up and say, "We need help."

So Hyde came into play. I attended and really began communicating with my parents. I saw my Dad ask for help, and really look at himself with his own issues, and that is when it all clicked for me. To see a man who had given me everything ask for help inspired me to do some «digging» in myself. He let his guard down and let us all in. I felt closer to my Dad than anyone else in the world. I am thankful he took that step and led the way. I did this also, but the snowball starting rolling in my family when he took the risk.

Today as a twenty-five-year old, I'm trying to figure out what life has got in stock for me. I still turn to my parents for guidance—two people I can count on to support me and give me strength in times of need. I feel as though I have been given a torch to light my way, and the journey is in progress. I'm not exactly sure where the path is leading me, but I feel I have the right crew with me, and the right attitude to get there.

I'm grateful I was blessed with this family, and grateful we had Hyde to help us figure some things out. I learned a million things along the way, and one of the most important ones is that emotional honesty and letting go is a gateway to real communication. It has helped my family and me tenfold, and it started with my father.

Youngest brother Robert writes:

I've always been really close with my parents, although I didn't receive the most attention. My brothers, especially Mike, did garner more attention. He was pretty rebellious, and I was the quiet one who tried not to cause unneeded problems.

I always had a strong bond with my mom because of how loving she was. She made sure I did my chores, homework, and kept my room clean. But she told me she loved me every day, and I always knew she loved me and my brothers equally.

She went to every sporting event I had growing up, told me she was proud of me, and made sure I was doing my best in everything. My dad and I also had a very close bond. My mom always tells me that I am so much like him, and I guess that is why we are so close.

I can remember wanting to be just like him growing up. I wanted to go to Notre Dame like him. He got me interested in sports, and I loved having him as my soccer coach. He worked a ton during the week, but made sure he was at my soccer practices and games. My brothers were my best friends and role models growing up. I followed in their footsteps in almost everything I did.

Hyde definitely helped strengthen the bonds within our family and helped me with my communication with my parents. I was very quiet and tried not to cause trouble, so I did not really share my issues with my parents. While I didn't have as many big issues to deal with as my brothers, I still had my own struggles.

Hyde taught me my issues were just as important as my brothers' and also helped me be a better big brother for my sister. I am very open with her, and I think she is very comfortable coming to me with her problems.

As we can see from these stories, the eldest brother's acting out brought the help that the family needed to address the NEDs of the parents and reaffirm the family bonds.

The Horton Family

The next family story helps us realize the depth of power that the Negative Love Syndrome has, not only upon our lives, but also upon the lives of those we love. From birth we seek the love of our parents; in this case, the mother as a child felt she needed to be nice, achieve, and be in the limelight to gain the love of her mother, but at the same time, be humble and stay in the background to gain the love of her father!

The resulting inner conflict within herself as to how she should act interfered with the expression of her own spirit, and in this process, distracted her from sharing her natural capacity to love with her children, thus interfering with the development of nature's bond with her children.

Mom writes:

There is a picture in my house—an actual black and white photograph by a well-known artist— of his nine- or ten-year-old daughter, feeding pigeons in a piazza in Italy, her arms out, bread crumbs in her hands, and several pigeons walking up and down her arms. There are dozens of birds all around her on the ground.

I was drawn to the photo and bought it because of the expression on the girl's face. To me she is saying, "Whoa, look at this! Bring it on!" I feel her spirit as she is so excited at what she has accomplished in attracting all these pigeons. It's a spirit that I always felt was inside me, but I struggled to let it out as a little girl. It's a spirit that in my mind was the opposite of messages and instructions that I got from my parents: "Be sweet; be nice; don't be angry, be perfect."

I was the second child born into a middle-class family of Irish and German /French descent. We lived in a small town in western Pennsylvania; my maternal grandparents lived seven miles away and my paternal grandparents a block away.

My mother was the oldest of thirteen children; she was "mothering" by the time she was five. She told me "there was always a baby on the way," and she was changing diapers and giving baths to her younger siblings. Her father, when he got angry, went into a rage, and she was at times hit with a belt, as were her siblings.

My father was the middle of three children; their family had a family business in the same small town where I grew up.

My parents married early; she was just nineteen and he eighteen. I was always perfectly dressed; my mother made almost all of my clothes, and I didn't just wear a pair of plaid slacks, I wore the slacks and the matching vest! I must have stood out in an unusual way. My mother loved clothes and loved dressing—both herself and me.

As a child, I was obedient, responsible, and sweet; I did most of what my parents told me to do, arguing little and obeying almost all the time. My brother was just the opposite: he argued, got in trouble, fought with my mother, and often begged my dad to get her off his back." I was afraid of that kind of relationship with my mother, so I chose to obey. "You should know what I want!" she would often say. She also enjoyed being in the limelight, and two "perfect" kids and a "perfect" household helped her with this.

I learned that I had to be responsible for keeping her happy; I had to do the right thing, and when I didn't, I certainly didn't want to let her know or get caught! I don't think I did do very much wrong; however, at times living felt like walking a tightrope, but I really didn't know anything different. My brother developed an ulcer his freshman year in college, and I got one when I was sixteen. My mother would joke that if she got the next ulcer, the problem would be due to my father, but if he got the next one, she would be the problem. Neither of them ever got an ulcer.

Image was important to my parents, especially to my mother. How you looked and what you said really mattered. I held a lot in. In high school, I was the model student, model cheerleader, and everyone liked me. I was voted homecoming queen and prom queen in the same year.

My boyfriends in college were never good enough for me, according to my parents—especially my mother. The phrase I remember was, "He's not strong enough for you." I never bothered to ask what she meant; I just kept dating him knowing that it would go nowhere eventually. My parents met my husband the day before our wedding; I was not taking any chances on my mother squashing this relationship.

So my mother was very controlling, a perfectionist, wanting the limelight, wanting her children perfect and in the limelight as well, while my father was a very quiet, humble man, who liked being in the background, never in the spotlight.

Wanting to be in the background and in the limelight were two very strong patterns in me from each of them and these patterns weren't very compatible!

After graduating I joined an international airline, as I had studied languages in college. That career was short-lived, for at the end of the third week of training, I met a good-looking fighter pilot and we married four months after we met. My transfer of bases to be closer to him was denied, so after only six months of flying, I resigned. My husband never asked me to do that; I thought it was what I should do to make him happy, so the pattern of thinking, "I should know what he wants," was still alive in me. We didn't talk about my decision; I thought I knew what he wanted.

We moved a lot—twenty-four times in total—some of them international moves. Again, it didn't matter whether I wanted to move; it was his job that required it and I just did what I thought was expected of me. I may have complained to friends that I was tired of moving, but I never would say that to him. I learned to bloom where I was planted— not a bad pattern to have adopted— probably from my parents who never wanted to make trouble for each other or for others.

After eighteen years of marriage and two sons, my family found itself in trouble. The symptom was an off-track teenager,

our first son. When we got to Hyde, I thought he was the prob-
lem, just like most parents who come to Hyde. I was okay, my
husband was okay. We didn't like each other very much, but we
were doing well by all the achievement categories—nice house,
nice cars, great vacations, etc. Never mind the fact that I was
a controlling mother (sound familiar?) who could not express
appropriate, direct anger. I had adopted that pattern, and was
serving it well! Never mind the fact that I wanted perfect chil-
dren so I could feel better about myself; never mind the fact
that my husband was never home, just climbing the corporate
ladder and avoiding all the problems at home, including me.
The problem was not us; it was the boy.

But I was the one who got us to Hyde. Despite the fact that
the truth of our story didn't look pretty or sound nice, I knew we
were in trouble and I started to tell. I told people who knew peo-
ple who knew someone who had gone to Hyde. When I couldn't
get my husband to agree to attend the interview, I left for a few
days until we made an agreement he would go to the interview.
Having a child who needs help brought out my "mother bear"
instincts: "I'll do whatever it takes to get this kid some help."

Hyde doesn't put up with the parents' assumption that it's
all about the kid; in fact, it was in the interview that I got a
glimpse that I might be part of the problem. I thought I was a
good parent, but I learned that I was not a responsible parent.
I was parenting as a duplication of my past, and my husband
was parenting as a reaction to his past. It was like we had six
parents in the house: my parents, his parents, and the two of
us! We had never discussed our parenting as a vision for what
we each wanted for our children, our family, and ourselves.

It was at Hyde that I first got a glimpse of all this. I could
not let on the truth with others because so often it didn't sound
nice. How could I "be sweet" and still say that I was sick of
moving? How could I look perfect and say that I was in an
unhappy marriage? How could I let out a spirit that was ready

to explode inside me and still be loyal to a father who was humble and in the background? And fighting that need to be in the background was an adopted trait from my mother who loved to be in the limelight!

The manifestation of this, and the time that I remember bringing this conflict into full consciousness, was one day in a Hyde parent workshop in which we were asked to look at those emotional dispositions, both productive and unproductive, that we got from each of our parents.

There was a list to choose from, and on the list were: "Don't notice me" and "Notice me!" I circled them both, and then realizing what I'd done, thought, "How can this be?" Then I realized it was true: I was wearing a tasteful, but noticeable, outfit complete with cowgirl boots, but I was sitting in a distant corner of the room, not wanting to be called on. At that moment I was very aware of the way these two traits were at war within me. I was also beginning to realize that looking good, as in appearance standards, was not supporting that inside spirit that I was aware of but had not yet named as "Bring it on, world!"

Hyde's slogan about "the truth will set you free" is very true. I began to watch for places in my life where I was repeating these two warring patterns, and they were frequent. I'd find myself thinking one thing, and toning down the way I said it so as not to rub anyone the wrong way. I'd get ready to present a workshop (part of my job at the time) and be as concerned about how people would accept my looks as I was about what I was teaching them. I'd want to express a feeling that wasn't "pretty" to someone close to me, and couldn't do it because it wasn't nice.

I think it was the realization of those two main contradictory dispositions in me, one from my father and one from my mother, which led me to the Hoffman Institute. The Hoffman homework brought out many, many more realizations; facing that homework was an enormous challenge as it felt so disloyal to look at my parents in that way and to admit that not all of what I was carrying from them was serving me well. Some of it was, but admitting to the not-so-productive was hard.

By the time I got to Hoffman, I was very excited about getting in touch with that spirit that had begun to emerge at Hyde. I had completed the homework and was ready to dig into finding myself. A friend had told me that it was a very spiritual process, and I had felt the same way about Hyde's process, so I was not afraid.

Hoffman allowed me to see where each of my parents learned the attitudes and traits they passed on to me, and where their parents learned them. I easily forgave them for things that I'd been blaming them for; it wasn't their fault! They'd done the best they knew how to do.

This then allowed me to focus on loving me, accepting me, being comfortable with me, and not fearing those things that didn't sound nice or look pretty or weren't perfect. What an amazing freedom in which to be able to say to myself, "Bring it on, world!"

As we read her husband's story, we can see her rebellion against her parent's patterns.

Dad writes:

The family dynamic I grew up in was laissez-faire. My formative years were spent overseas and we relocated on average every three years. My brother and I became adaptable, self-reliant. and largely responsible. We marvel today, that as blond-haired preteens we wandered the streets of Rio de Janeiro on our own.

We poached carp in the botanical gardens, rode clinging to the outsides of streetcars, and snuck out of Sunday school to bet on the horses at the Jockey Club in the poor people's section. *Though not aware of the details of our adventures, my parents were not detached or derelict in their parenting—they knew we were out on our own and when they sensed that we could handle it responsibly they gave us the room to learn on our own. Mind you, even Rio was a safer place back then.*

I liked my parents' way of parenting, and that's what I've emulated— superficially at least.

My wife's formative years could not have been more different than my own—basically small-town, conservative, grandparents nearby and involved, Girl Scouts, church and school leadership. Her parents were wonderful citizens, but were controlling and protective.

In the heat of our four-month courtship I don't remember giving any notice to the disparities in our upbringing, except that it was clear initially that my exotic background appealed to my wife.

But it wasn't long— maybe less than a year—before our twenty-year power struggle commenced: she trying to mold me into her selfless and settled father; and me forging a rootless, adventuresome lifestyle for us, while digging in to maintain my independence and fighting her set-agenda for the family.

So at age forty-five, what sort of person had I become? What was I modeling for my sons?

I now realize the boys would have sensed the power struggle between their parents, though I thought we were generally clandestine about it. In fact, they suspected greater rifts—fissures that I was not to learn about for years.

As a parent I thought I had mimicked my own, except I came to realize that some important elements were different or missing altogether in my version of it. They were laissez-faire but engaged; I was simply detached. They modeled values— compassion and courage chief among them; I had become so self-absorbed that my family was not a priority, and—though I had a history of risk-taking and physical courage—I lacked the courage to take a stand with a rebellious son and confront other family issues.

I'm not sure I modeled any principles or values at the time, but I for sure was a poster boy for achievement—I had a resume to die for. I soon came to realize that I was so respected for my past that I had stopped growing and it had given me the latitude to behave badly and get away with it.

And I wasn't alone as this sort of person in our affluent commuter suburb.

So we drop our two young boys—foreigners essentially after six years overseas (three years each in Sydney and Rio)—into a milieu of overcharged expectations and family dysfunction.

The older son—at the critical middle school age—had trouble adjusting. That his younger brother seemed to have an easier time probably didn't help. He was soon overwhelmed and then had a spectacular crash.

The shock and seriousness of it caused us to take stock as individuals and regroup as a family. Had we not, I hate to ponder where the four of us would be now.

It was inspiring to observe this family, struggling with their NED issues, then finally caught in the achievement culture, transform itself into a Hyde family, thanks to the leadership of the mother. She left the home until her husband agreed to come to the interview as the first step, and then I marveled at how well Dad then committed himself to doing his part to make the program work for the family.

It took two years for their son to join his parents in this transformation, but once he did, they were able to create real parent-child family bonds. The other son went on to become an all-American lacrosse player in college, but faced his struggles after college.

As I write this, the Hyde son graduated from college, launched a successful career, and is married with two children.

The Hyde son's take on his growing up experience:

My "bond" with my mom became stronger over time during my Hyde years. It was not a single event that turned things around in our relationship.

As you are well aware, I entered Hyde unwillingly, and since my mom was the biggest proponent for me going to Hyde, she became my biggest enemy at the time. It took over two years for me to buy into what Hyde was trying to teach—and my mom stood tough the entire time—not quitting on me but at the same time having the courage to take a hard look at her own issues and how those issues might have contributed to the dysfunction in our family.

I think that once I was willing to do the same—look at myself and what I needed to work on— it gave me an appreciation and a really strong sense of respect for my mom's toughness and her commitment to me and our family. I did not realize it at the time, but in retrospect, because she was willing to let me fail, not prop me up, not come to the rescue when I was down, this forced me to make a decision—sink or swim ...

We can understand the struggle of the son, who had been caught in the battle of wills of his parents; on one hand wanting to be true to the independent spirit of his father, and on the other, wanting the support of his mother. As Hyde helped his parents address their NEDs, he becomes free to "sink or swim" on his own.

*

In this chapter, we were introduced to two mothers of strong character, who were very committed to their children. Yet they failed to build the parent-child bond with their first child, and in fact, reached a point of desperation where they felt something was terribly wrong in preparing their children for life—something beyond their control.

What they did not comprehend was their profound attachment to how they themselves were raised. In seeking their parents' love as children, they both had controlling mothers, and therefore internalized love for their children that was expressed by trying to control their lives—in a good way, of course. That meant helping everything turn out right for them.

To the child, that is a very mixed blessing. It means that with every anxiety, uncertainty, roadblock, adversity, challenge, failure, calamity, etc., support will always be there. However, the cost to the child is self-confidence, independence, initiative, and vision.

So the child begins a love-resentment relationship with the parent. The child can't help wanting the security of the parent always being there to help clean up the messes, problems or failures, but at the same time, at a deeper level, the child resents the parent for controlling his/her life and not preparing him/her to be self-sufficient.

For kids with spirit—like the two in this chapter—this non-addressing of the parent's NED (or need to control) usually leads them to act more recklessly, to join the fast crowd, and to get into situations beyond parental control. It's the only way they feel they can get some control of their lives. And in the achievement culture, the fast crowd keeps getting larger and offering more opportunities to rebel.

In order to develop the parent-child bond, this is why it is so critical that we parents continually work to increase our children's responsibility for their own growth until they reach primary self-sufficiency about age nineteen. We essentially must increase our children's self-sufficiency from zero percent to fifty-one percent in just 19 years.

There are steps children take in gaining responsibility, the stage when they manage lemonade stands, for example. They also learn much about responsibility from daily household chores and community service projects. We make them own up to mistakes, lies, and other character flaws. If we really look for the opportunities to teach our children personal responsibility, we will find them.

We are first a mentor to our children. As a mentor, we must come to understand the unique nature and learning style of children to be effective and gain their trust. But ultimately, the trust is based on our doing what we believe is the right thing for our children's future, regardless of how our children feel about it—as we saw in this last story. The family transformation occurred because the mother was willing to leave home to get her husband and son to Hyde; she then put up with two years of her son feeling she was the enemy.

Of course, if we are generally making the right decisions in slowly but steadily transferring the responsibility to our child over those first nineteen years, then the bond will steadily build and there is no need for real conflict. But it is reassuring to observe that when a parent has the right commitment to a child, it can be powerful enough to overcome dysfunctions or off-track situations of a family, as it did in this last example.

Chapter 8

More Examples

The last chapter revealed what happens to the parent-child bond when parents simply pass on the negative emotional dispositions (NEDs) and Negative Love Syndrome they internalized in childhood from their parents. But suppose they recognize this, and rebel against these negative patterns? What is the affect on their children? The next family story gives such an example:

The Wilson Family

The mother writes:

Within me were equal measures of anticipation and dread when I arrived at the Hoffman Process that hot summer day. I'd been eager to experience it for a number of years (several friends had recommended it) but also knew I was in for an intense level of self-scrutiny bound to be sometimes painful. Still, at sixty, I was ready for a jolt of life.

The pre-process work had gotten me thinking about the negative patterns in my childhood and adulthood. I'd become very good, actually, at discussing them; transcending or ridding myself of them would be a whole new thing.

Those negative patterns had grown from a life of privilege on the outside, emptiness on the inside. Both of my parents were born dirt poor in the South. My father, one of those "up from the boot straps" stories, used his guts and wits to excel in college, in WWII, in his journalism career and at his post at the Pentagon. My mother, his intellectual equal, complemented him beautifully and dutifully from the start of their relationship at the University of Georgia.

Through the years, their love was a tight, closed circle that even their children could never penetrate. Our job was to succeed, as they did, and achieve our dreams, whatever they were. Everything else was secondary. Hugs and kisses, emotions of any kind other than happiness, were not permitted. If I was sad or started to cry, I would be sent to my room with my "emotional indulgence." If I said that I was nervous about a test in school or weekend date, "No you're not," my mother would correct me: "Smiths don't have nerves."

The message at home was simple: To be useful was the point of life. Little else was of value. So I grew up, the youngest of three daughters, focused on accomplishments, the outcome of efforts, while downplaying or denying how things felt or what was going on (like my mother's drinking too much.) By nature intuitive and emotional, this was a struggle for me. I always felt like I was in the wrong family. I longed for warm, close-knit talks and experiences. I got brief chats or worse, mockery when I'd ask questions.

*

I had raised my own two children pretty much in opposition to how I was raised. My parents were strict and sometimes military. We had to say "Yes, Ma'am" or "Yes, Sir," when addressing them, and before leaving on a family outing, Daddy would call out, "March Order!" and we daughters would line up at the front door. My children, in contrast, could negotiate almost anything with me. There were few rules. My son and daughter helped me make decisions, which often resulted in them doing whatever they wanted—in their early teens, for example, staying out too late, constantly using the phone, and in the case of my son, leading his close group of friends into truancy, pot-smoking, and such. I was too busy distinguishing myself in my journalism career (and accumulating resentments against my husband) to pay much attention.

My husband and I were separated, and barely talking except about our son and the destructive path he was on. After stints in both day and residential rehab failed to "fix" him, we knew we had to change his environment. We found Hyde School, where it was pointed out to us that our son's situation was a reflection of our attitudes and choices in life. Were we willing to look at ourselves while our son took responsibility for himself? Yes, we were.

It took a year or more for me to see how my focus on achievement and my emotional absence (physical, too) from my children (and husband) had been part of why they sought deep connections elsewhere. I also began to see how I had labeled them "the bad kid" (son) and "good kid" (daughter,) neither of which was true! I had done it to find answers that would let me avoid looking inside myself. Now I wanted to find the truth, whatever it was, and Hyde offered our family this opportunity.

After two years, my husband and I reconciled and saw how we had both been so busy on our career treadmills that we had lost our family. We decided to recommit to each other and to our family. We enrolled our daughter at Hyde, and happily accepted jobs there. Although my background had been twenty-five years in journalism, I joined Hyde's Family Learning Center, where I could talk with parents and students alike, learning from them and sharing my own experiences.

Even more important, Hyde would be a place where I could continue (with other people) my journey of personal growth. With other parents, I could work on myself and keep trying to figure out why I judge myself so harshly and why I constantly, secretly put myself down.

So it was with about fourteen years of Hyde's self-discovery experience that I signed up for the Hoffman Process. One thing I knew for sure as I unpacked my suitcase of summer T-shirts: I want to stop putting my negative patterns on my children. I've done enough of that already.

*

At Hoffman I expected to face the demons that had nestled deep down in me. The one I most feared was the voice that judged "bad Cathy!" if I did or said the wrong thing, or felt an emotion or spent time relaxing instead doing useful things. I'd become an expert at pushing down my feelings and getting most of my rewards through work, not other people. I'd learned early to never express anger; instead I would turn it into tears and then hide in my room, feeling confused and unworthy of interaction.

Well, face demons I did.

On Hoffman Process Day Three or Four I found myself—for the first time ever—letting out anger toward my parents. "I'm mad, not sad!" I screamed as I bashed at the hurt and confusion I had felt as a child. "Liar!" I yelled, "I <u>do</u> have nerves! People have feelings!" It took every ounce of courage I had in me to own these feelings that I had buried so far into my soul. I was exhausted when the exercise was over. But I felt—for the first time ever —free of a pattern that had continued a negative influence on me, (and on my children,) long after my parents were gone from my everyday life.

On another day, I delved deeply into what my parents' childhoods were like, and where their attitudes and behavior patterns had come from. I remembered how my mother's mother had died when my mother was just two years old and how she had spent her girlhood moving from one aunt to another, never fully attaching emotionally to anyone, lest she be yanked away, as was the routine. I remembered how my father was pressured as a young boy that he was the only person who could "save" his family from the tragedy of the Great Depression that was all around him.

Later, the Hoffman Process helped me to appreciate my parents and feel compassion for them. I saw how my mother had experienced abandonment, and thus learned self-preservation. It meant staying remote. I saw how my father, called upon to save his family, felt he had to succeed or else. There was no choice for him, no time for frivolity or emotion. My parents weren't taught to deal with or accept emotion; they were taught to hide it. Except in their closed, intimate circle, they weren't taught to love themselves, so they didn't know how to teach me to love myself. They only knew how to hold me to high standards. And I'm grateful for that.

With this new understanding of how they had handled pain and negativity in their lives, I understood them in an inspiring new way. The love I felt for them was deeper than ever, and I felt this great love not just for my parents but for my entire family and for all the people in my life.

Today I see we are all struggling to live with more love and compassion in our lives. We have all hurt others and been hurt, and we all want forgiveness and to understand one another. That is what I believe with all my heart. And that is what I'm striving to do now, every day, as best I can.

The biggest NED Mom has to address in her own life is her parent's totally misguided ban on her feelings as "emotional indulgences" while she was growing up. While perhaps understandable, since her parents were in a survival mentality, this parental attitude was destructive to the development of their children's self-confidence.

We gain far more sense of self-worth from expressing our emotions and feelings than we do from the qualities that produce our achievements. Mom was a Pulitzer prize winner, and yet when she went to Hoffman, she was still carrying a mental picture of "bad Cathy!" in her mind.

But as Mom says, *"I had raised my own two children pretty much in opposition to how I was raised."* So just like parents who get caught in the pattern of raising children as they were raised— as we saw in Chapter 6—so was Mom choosing a pattern based on her childhood experience to raise her children.

The problem with this is such patterns and experiences are alien to our children. Our children are not us; regardless of what genes we may share with them. They are unique individuals gifted with a unique potential. We are truly unique parents, gifted with unique parenting instincts. The creative human growth process is based on uniting these two unique partners into a parent-child bond. Of course this bond will be influenced by the other parent and ultimately by our family. But the basic parent-child bond is a unique relationship that is developed over the years.

The problem with parents utilizing patterns in raising children is they are injecting experiences into the process that the children cannot identify with or understand. It makes sense to the parent but not to the child. However if the parent will focus on developing the parent-child bond, some of the lessons the parent learned in childhood will then fit nicely into this relationship.

Son Jay writes:

Growing up both of my parents were always committed to their careers. When I decided (or someone decided) that I should join the Cub Scout troop in Boston where we lived, my mother took on the role of the Den Mother. My mom who was leading a staff of editors and writers at one of the largest newspapers in the country would come home from work and put on a Cub Scout uniform—complete with hat and handkerchief! I never fully understood or appreciated the sacrifices my mother made at the time, but the bond we shared from the beginning was as solid as iron.

The bond between my mother and me allowed us both to put our guard down and be comfortable, safe, and happy. My mom created the space for me to do that and as a result we shared the closest of family ties.

Later in New Jersey, like any adolescent, I would strike out on my own socially, looking to create my own new relationships, community, and fun. I would show my parents that I didn't need their guidance or even their love.

The more I ventured out on my own and made my own choices, the more my mother tried to tighten her grasp. I was pushing her away and the harder I pushed, the tighter she would try to squeeze. That push and pull created a firestorm between us. My mom went through what I affectionately refer to as: "The RAMBO-MOM years." I picture my mom out on our lovely front porch in suburban New Jersey, not watering the garden or reading a book, but waiting with gritted teeth and a sawed-off shotgun for her son and his cronies to return home so that she might inflict some accountability and order in my life. (I'm exaggerating of course— but not by much!)

I guess our bond was so strong that my mother just couldn't let me make my own decisions or my own mistakes. Maybe it hurt her too much to see that I would be making many mistakes.

For my part, my parents built such strong relationships with me that I was just "too big for my britches" as my father once put it. While I lacked some confidence in some areas of my life, and I didn't trust or believe fully in myself, I was overly confident in my ability to accomplish and to achieve whatever I wanted to. I didn't realize how hard I would have to work to reach those accomplishments. I needed to fall on my face a few times, I needed to feel failure, and I needed to learn how to work hard without my parents doing it all.

So, for some time our bond was broken. We both seemed to be depressed during those years and our relationship became frozen and pretty adversarial.

In my desk drawer I keep a photograph that my father took when I was seventeen. It's a view from our front porch in New Jersey. There are three police cars in front of our house. Like they say: A picture is worth a thousand words. My father snapped the shot on the morning my parents would tell me that I was going to boarding school at Hyde School in Maine.

The fact that my mother called in a favor from her buddy, the chief of police, and had three police cars show up before I was even awake was a reflection of just how bad my attitude could get. My mother's move was also a reflection of how over-the-top and reactionary my mom could be. The fact that my father went out on the porch and took pictures sort of reflects the space he was in.

Luckily for my whole family, I did go to Hyde. The distance between my parents and me was one thing, but the commitment I witnessed in my parents to be involved in the school and to challenge themselves in the same ways that I was being challenged was a game-changer. Finally my parents were given the space and direction to look deeply at themselves and to start moving toward their own goals.

The time we spent as a family at Hyde School set the table for my adult relationship with my mother. It was when she stopped being the primary investor in my life and started to invest fully in her own. Now we are both lucky to have the relationship that we do. It's not mired in worry, control, or disappointment. We have the same bond we've always had, but as two adults, we are *completely honest with one another, we can tell each other the truth (regardless of how hard it might be to hear), and as always (maybe most importantly) we can laugh together.*

As Mom raises Jay in opposition to how she was raised, he feels a bond with his mother, but he does not see her as a mentor: *I would show my parents I didn't need their guidance or even their love.* Then when Mom finally does take control, Jay calls it the "RAMBO-MOM years," explaining to me he thought she was crazy. It isn't until he gets to Hyde when he sees both himself and his parents being challenged in the same ways does it become a "game-changer" for him, and their deeper bond is discovered.

To review the situation, Mom's parents taught her some very strong principles, but in the process, passed on some very strong NEDs to her. Mom sought to correct the NEDs, and as her son hit the challenges of adolescence, realized she was throwing the baby out with the bath water, and sought to correct the situation by coming to Hyde.

As a high-expectation family, they have their ups and downs but keep moving in a positive direction. They are a very close family today, but given the power of NEDs in high-expectation families, it is my guess that Jay will not fully appreciate the dramatic transformation in his parents until his own children become teenagers.

I say this because Mom acknowledges that in rebellion to her own parents, she did not mentor her children to the degree that she should have. But when she sought to correct it, Jay even today refers to it as the "RAMBO-MOM years." So how will he mentor his own children?

Jay's sister Sylvia writes:

This "assignment" brought up a lot of emotions for me, things that I have always thought of as in the past. Resentments and hurts from childhood that I truly considered water under the bridge came up in a big way. Mostly reading what my mom wrote made me feel very sad.

What brought about the sadness was feeling quite absent within my family as a child and adolescent, especially as Jay's "issues" required more and more attention from my parents. I felt unimportant, invaluable, and invisible. What my mother wrote brought those feelings right back. It alarmed me because I really have felt at peace with my childhood and adolescence, always thanking Hyde for giving my family the opportunity to work through those issues, and in doing so, leaving them behind us. In regards to a parent-child bond, I'm really not sure I felt it strongly with my parents until after I graduated from Hyde. My relationship with my parents is closer now than it probably has ever been, and we get closer as time goes on. As a child, I felt the most deeply bonded and connected to my brother. He was the constant person in my life who made me feel safe and happy. When we were growing up, both of our parents worked a lot.

Interestingly, it is Jay with whom I now feel the most disconnected. I have very strong bonds with my mom and my dad, we communicate openly, honestly, and regularly. They know what is going on with me and my life and they support me. They are always there for me. I'm not sure when this bond solidified, but I feel like it happened after I graduated from Hyde in the wake of some traumatic experiences that I had. Hyde brought us together and helped us to address the past, but the strong bond I have with them now developed later on, in my twenties.

Sylvia's comments are very helpful. I've always said the "good kid" in the family needs the Hyde experience even more than the "off-track kid." "Off-track" kids fully express themselves, both good and bad, which get their parents' full attention, while the "good kids" carefully monitor their behavior and performance, and thus don't get any additional attention. But kids are born with a spirit, and if they have the courage to express it, adults sometimes aren't going to like it.

The more problems Jay had, the more Sylvia got pushed into the background. Since Jay in essence had control of the house, his concern for Sylvia could make her feel "safe and happy." However her parents were feeling like failures as parents, so their main concern was Jay. But now Sylvia's parents have transformed themselves and their parenting and Jay has his own family, so it is understandable that Sylvia became more connected to her parents.

Sylvia reminds us that "good kids" go through the struggles and pain of all kids; they just hide it because they are not expected to have problems. Since none of us like pain, it's easy for our minds to forget painful experiences in our childhood. But our hearts and souls always remember them, thus they profoundly affect our lives, without our knowing it.

So when Sylvia talks about the traumatic experiences she had after she graduated from Hyde, much of the trauma may be built on the struggles and pain she had kept to herself in childhood. As mentioned by a "good kid" earlier—"Hyde taught me my issues were just as important as my brother's."— Sylvia needed as much individual attention as Jay did.

Dad writes:

The family bond shared by the four of us has been present as far back as I can remember. But, for a period of time, it became hidden, obscured. I was unable to access its strength and comfort. It was so distant that I thought it might have disappeared for good. Over several years, I had felt increasingly isolated, angry, and afraid. I think each of us did. This obscured our bond even further, and our family was no longer a safe environment to address counter-productive attitudes or share our personal struggles.

Thankfully, Cathy and I worked together and found Hyde School—a place that offered our family an opportunity for positive change.

In 1996, we became a Hyde family when Jay enrolled as a junior. Sylvia enrolled as a junior in 1998. Hyde School was as valuable an experience for Cathy and me as it was for our children.

The family learning program at Hyde provided a safe process for the four of us to share our struggles and fears. The more we listened to each other identify personal struggles, the safer we felt to openly share our own. In our case, this brought us closer. It was a path to personal and family growth. The challenges and the learning continue. But, most of the time, they serve to enrich our family bond. It is present and very powerful.

Dad very nicely summaries the Wilsons' experience at Hyde and the overall progress as a family.

Cathy Wilson was highly respected as a journalist, highlighted by winning a Pulitzer Prize for her work. Her writing above shows how she worked to marry her integrity and high standards with her natural capacity to love, which has helped to unify their family bond.

*

What about children in families who become immersed in dysfunction? We might initially think these kids are at a distinct disadvantage in life because of the increased negative patterns they seemingly would experience. But we should remember the Friedrich Nietzsche quote, *What does not kill me, makes me stronger.*

Certainly we have seen many outstanding individuals in life emerge from very dysfunctional households—as pointed out in the book *Cradles of Eminence—Childhoods of more than 700 famous men and women,* by Victor Goertzel and Mildred George

Goertzel (1964: updated second edition, Great Potential Press, 2004)

Why do dysfunctional households break some kids, and then make other ones?

It is both my personal and teaching experience that kids reach a point of truth where they must stand up for themselves if they are going to become independent and self-reliant individuals. And if they do in fact stand up for themselves, I believe they will get the help they need.

This happened to me when I finally stood up to my stepfather when I was thirteen. At the time he dominated my life; I couldn't seem to do anything right. I had a huge inferiority complex; I was a coward, backing down from bullies. I was miserable. Then one night he was unfair to me, and I said to myself, "Joe, if you don't stand up for yourself now, maybe you never will. So I went to my room, took out a piece of paper, and wrote, "Dear Dad." I was going to ask my biological father if I could come and live with him.

Then reality hit me. He doesn't want me. And I would be leaving my mother, the core of my growth, and my stepfather, who, in spite of the unfairness, was helping me grow. I sat there helplessly and said to myself, "I'm just a little kid, and I can't even stand up for myself." I put my head on the desk and started crying uncontrollably.

Then, a presence entered the room and communicated, "But you did stand up for yourself, and saw it was better for you to stay here."

I sat silently for a while, wondering if this really happened, or if my mind dreamed it up. But the logic was right; I would have left if Dad would have me. I wasn't playing games, but I wasn't going to wait for a long letter explaining why he couldn't take me in.

In the end, I believed it all happened. This helped me begin to stand up for myself, deal with my cowardice, face bullies, and begin to develop self-confidence. I've had two experiences like that since in my life and have come to realize that it doesn't make any difference whether they actually happened, or if it was my conscience speaking to me, or if I simply dreamed them up. The only important thing is I believed in them, and following my belief has helped make me the person I am today.

The Cohen Family

In the following story, we observe the little girl Lisa become the helpless victim of dysfunctional parents, even sexual abuse. But in spite of all the adjustments she has to make to the dysfunctions and negative patterns in her life, we are aware of her inner strength, which finally expresses itself when Lisa sees an opportunity to change her life by attending Hyde.

Mom writes:

My mother was raised in a home where she was an outsider. She and her older sister were born before my grandparents were married in the late 1930s. They were raised as the bad seed of the family. After my grandparents were married they had three more children who were the golden children. My mother and her older sister spent most of their childhood trying to fit into this dysfunction. Their father was an active alcoholic and their mother a narcissistic hypochondriac. My mother responded to this pressure by looking for acceptance wherever she could find it, usually with boys. Her sister went to the other extreme, becoming the best daughter she could be under the circumstances. She excelled in school, working hard to prove her worth. Neither of these approaches worked as they could not change the one thing that made them different: being born out of wedlock.

When my mother left home at seventeen, she was determined to get as far away as possible. She still sought acceptance by continuing her promiscuous ways. Through adulthood she married four times, had five children and also numerous affairs. Three of us were born of the marriages, while the other two were products of affairs. My mother raised us in the only way she thought would work: a lot of screaming and a lot of smacking; sometimes all out beatings.

She loved us though. She wanted for us what she didn't have: a house, out of the city where we could live a "normal" life. She married her last husband for this very reason. He promised to buy her a house and accepted her five children. We moved into this house when I was six. Her new husband soon emerged as a pedophile with me as his victim. Our home was one of chaos and self-survival. My mother worked long hours, so we were left to our own devices a lot. This allowed my stepfather free reign. He came into my room at night for three years.

I was confused and scared most of the time. Trying to make sense of where I fit in this family, I took on whatever I could to feel love. My role was one of little mother, Miss Responsible. I thought if I became needed my mother might like me a little. She told me of a time when I asked her if I should change my name so she would like me more. This was a turning point for her. Somehow this woke her up to what was happening and she entered intensive therapy and finally threw my stepfather out of the house when I was nine.

I was twelve when I finally told my mother about my stepfather. She had finally reached a place where I felt like I could tell her and not be judged by her. I was sent to a therapist immediately. It was so successful for my mother she couldn't imagine it would not work for me. It was awful. My therapist did not know how to deal with abused children, and I left more confused then when I entered. To add to this confusion, my father, who I had never really met, showed up when I was thirteen to meet me and my brother. It was odd and confusing.

I was not sure how I was supposed to respond. I was excited and wanted the connection, but I felt disloyal to my mother because he was quite abusive to her in their marriage. I was torn to say the least. He promised to write every week and left with his new wife and kids. He wrote twice, and I never heard from him again.

The next few years continued my need to fit in and be accepted. I went to a trade school and joined the carpentry program because my mother wanted me to. I was the only girl in this program and really did not enjoy it. I excelled in academics. It was something I had complete control over and I enjoyed the positive attention it gave me. My mother continued her journey of self-discovery and our home life settled considerably. She began to look for a way to help my younger brother do better in school. He was struggling academically. A friend who sent her kids to Hyde told her she should check it out.

My brother entered Hyde in his junior year I attended his family weekend. My mother was not happy with the way things were going for my brother as his learning disabilities continued. I knew however that this was a place I wanted to be. They were talking about things that spoke to my soul. Who are you? No really ... who are you at your core? I convinced my mother to let me interview. After a six-hour interview I was accepted and enrolled in January of my junior year. My mother had made the ultimate financial sacrifice and sold our house so that I could go.

After three weeks I decided I wanted to go home. I was so used to going unnoticed that I was very uncomfortable with all the attention I was getting. My teachers wanted to know what risks I was taking to challenge myself, what about my relationship with my mother needed to change, why I was such a people pleaser. This was far too intimate for me. I wanted out. I wanted to return to my invisible existence where I could control who paid attention and who didn't.

I called my mother and expected she would come and get me because she was unhappy with Hyde. I was wrong. She told me that since I started this I needed to finish it. A friend of mine and I planned to run away. I had someone at home that was going to come and pick us up. When it came time I just couldn't do it. Either fear or a need to prove I could do it, I am not sure. I do know that once I backed out of running away I put all my efforts into being the best Hyde student I could be. I excelled in leadership and academics. At the end of the year I was told I needed another year before I could be a senior at Hyde. That was it for my mother. My brother did not return to Hyde and she told me if I wanted to she would pay for just one more year and would not participate in the family program. She was done.

I chose to return. I knew I needed to not be at home if I wanted to break the chain of dysfunction that was my family's legacy. I spent the next two years at Hyde learning who I was and feeling very grateful for the opportunity. Interestingly this fed my people-pleaser tendencies more than I was aware. I played the same role as I did in my family, ultra responsible, willing to fulfill any request for help I could. My Advanced Junior year was one that built my confidence and helped me to begin to deal with the abuse of my childhood. I was able to trust enough to begin to talk about it and look at what role it was playing in my life and relationships.

To come back for a senior year I worked in a plastics factory full time for a summer so I could show Hyde that my commitment was worth a financial aid investment. The money I made went to Hyde and they granted me the rest in scholarship. By the time I graduated I had learned the value of standing for what I needed, as was the case of coming back to Hyde for my senior year. My mother was not involved in my Hyde experience, but I knew I had to be there. When I graduated I felt like

I could conquer whatever the world threw at me. I told veteran teacher Paul Hurd I would be back to work in twenty years.

By the time I came to work at Hyde, fifteen years later, I had four children of my own. I was convinced that I would not pass on the same dysfunction I had grown up with. I would explain every decision I made to the kids. Negotiation was the name of the game. I would want them to understand why I was disciplining them, and further I wanted them to agree with the accountability. If they didn't agree I would either lower the bar or move them into agreement through an angry outburst. I handled my marriage much the same way. I wanted everyone to be happy but I was the only gauge of that happiness.

Working through the parent program at Hyde with my kids, I have come to realize that the old patterns from my childhood had indeed been passed on. My kids never knew which mom was going to be there: the agreeable negotiator or the sarcastic angry one. They were always trying to please me or rebel against my controlling ways. I was growing, but slowly. At work I spent a lot of my time over extending myself in order not to disappoint anyone. It was exhausting.

In a Hyde seminar, another parent thought I was willing to compromise my integrity to keep my marriage together. I was really angry, but knew at a deep level it was true. I had to take a good long look at what I was teaching my kids about relationships and knew we had to change.

This was followed by another session with the founder who told me I needed to let go of my mother in order to be the woman of my house. Again I knew this was the truth. As I began to make the necessary changes, I could see that my kids were proud of me. They began pushing me, and stopped seeing me as too fragile to handle hard truths. Hyde helped me see that if I am not taking steps in my growth, I am giving my kids permission to stay stuck as well.

It became clear when my marriage ended in divorce that something needed to change. I was told about the Hoffman Process and had seen the deep impact it had on a friend of mine. I signed up with great excitement that quickly turned to apprehension as I completed the extensive homework that pointed out the patterns I had adopted or rebelled against in my parents. I was shocked to see that although I was aware of my deep-seeded attitudes due to fourteen years on the Hyde faculty, I was only aware of them, but I was not transcending them. That is where my apprehension began.

The first night was a clear indication that this was going to be a long eight days as I fought the process. I could not surrender to it. The bittersweet ceremony left me feeling angry. I felt like I had been set up or that it was all fake. I realized later that this is how I felt when my mother would say she loved me and then hit me for no reason. I could never understand or trust where she was coming from.

It wasn't until the day we worked on our fathers that I hit a turning point. I was so sure that I only needed to work on my patterns I had gotten from my mother that I didn't give the work on my father much thought. When we went through the exercise it became clear that this had been a hidden issue for me. My dad left when I was eighteen months old, and I came to realize that I was desperate for someone in my life that would protect me and keep me safe. I had a profound reaction to the exercise and began to appreciate what this process was offering me. It was my way into who I was at the deepest level and a return to the joy of loving myself. I surrendered after this exercise and never looked back. I learned how to appreciate both my parents and understand that although they were at fault, they were not to blame because they too had patterns from their parents.

I participated in Hoffman over a year ago and the results are still with me. I can return to a place of serenity in a moment and I feel lighter and more joyful than I have all my life.

While Lisa was a student at Hyde, we could predict the problems she would ultimately have in her parenting, because her mother ultimately refused to participate in the Hyde family program. This meant the NEDs Lisa's mother experienced were never dealt with, and thus those NEDs were bound to reappear in Lisa's parenting.

Dad writes:

I always thought my family was very supportive and loving. My two sisters and I were brought up in a reform Jewish home. I was always told to try and not quit at whatever I was doing. We did not swear in the house, and if we lied, the paddle came out.

The family always seemed to be getting along and there never seemed to be anything wrong. If there was a problem in the family, Mom would handle it and not tell Dad. Seeing this dishonesty go on for years made me not want to deal with problems, and later I let my wife handle them. If I didn't know about the problems then I wouldn't have to deal with them.

I got in trouble for many things my dad didn't know about. Mom was the easy one to talk to; I just had to remember not to quit or lie. Mom and Dad always seemed to be very dependent on each other for everything.

When I was fifteen I was molested by a kid at school. I kept this secret because of shame. I became withdrawn and did not excel anymore. I started to screw up in classes.

We had to look good to the outside world. The time I got into trouble with the police, Dad bailed me out. I'm not sure what he did to make the problem go away, but I was grateful. Not sure what I learned, other than parents make problems go away. I decided that I wanted more for myself, I needed help and I was not getting it at home. There seemed to be too many secrets from us kids.

Dad was in a car accident, a child was killed, and the family blamed him. This tore him apart, and when asked about it, the answer was "no problem." That seemed to be the answer I was getting from both parents. We did not find out why Dad became so withdrawn, their fights started to get worse, and the support seemed fake.

I was constantly told all I had to do was my best and everything would work out. This is how I learned to be codependent on my wife as much as I was. I also thought all I had to do was push my kids, make sure they didn't quit and everything would work out.

So, support the kids, look good, fix problems and everything would be okay. This is how I took care of my kids and family. If a problem came up, I did not have to handle it as long as my wife did. This put real pressure on her and seemed to lead to our divorce. Being so codependent on each other we were suffocating each other, and this is what I was teaching my kids. I saw how it hurt my parents and now I was doing the same thing to my family.

While I was going to Hyde as a student, my parents showed up when needed, supporting the school and me. But at home it seemed to be the same when it came to them working with each other. Then I got into some real trouble with Hyde, and I asked my parents what to do. For the first time they just said, "We support you, but you have to deal with the problem." This was the first time I felt my parents really got something out of Hyde and maybe something I wanted to be like them in my parenting.

Working at Hyde when our kids were still young, I relied on my wife for everything. I was right, and if I didn't want to talk about something, I didn't. This was not a good marriage and this is what I was teaching my kids: Okay to fight behind closed doors and only talk about what I had to in public so the family looked good. My kids better get it right—keep problems in the house and if I didn't want to talk about something hard, then I didn't have to. Honesty and openness were not there, yet I thought they were.

What was I teaching my kids? What was I doing differently from what my parents did for me?

But there was a day at Hyde I felt Dad and I came together, when he talked about how he felt after the accident. It had taken him years to talk and share his feelings. I felt so close to him as he showed me how he could open up about something so deep within him. I saw him cry and it made me see he was not just the hard-ass I thought he was, but that it was okay to open up and share with others. That is when I finally told him about what happened to me at fifteen..

When I looked back on that seminar, I drew strength from it, which allowed me to tell my kids about being molested, and that it is okay to be open and share deep feelings with the family. I was trying so hard to look good at all costs, and it cost me my marriage.

Mom and Dad stayed together because of us kids, yet I was doing the same thing, and I did not want to be like them in this regard. But it was too late; my relationship with the kids was growing apart, and I was not sure what I was showing them.

When I entered the Hyde parent program, I was closed and not willing to be vulnerable. Then my wife and I divorced and I knew it was time to really look at myself. As each family weekend and FLC came and went, I became more and more open with my kids. I was able to face my fear of heights with my daughter; being on that ropes course for fifty minutes and to have her look up to me and say, "We support each other, you can face your fears." This is what Hyde taught us.

Facing my fears and being open helped me grow a stronger bond with each of my kids and my wife. After three years of divorce, we got remarried. Having Hyde in the family helped me see I cannot do it alone, that I need her and the kids to be part of the family.

Being able to open up and share my fears allowed me to show the kids how I too struggle with life—diabetes, heights, and spiders—being open allows us all to be vulnerable. "Don't quit and don't lie" have made my parenting stronger. My son got into trouble with the law. I reflected on my parents; I am here to help and support you, but you must face the problem head-on. He did, and it worked out fine.

Hyde taught me to let go of outcomes with the family and just follow where the truth takes us. This belief I got from Hyde, helped me deal with my issues, which allowed my wife and me to remarry. Each child is different and the support is always the same. They will make mistakes and I learned that I cannot fix it for them, but I can help and listen when they come to me.

Hyde has shown me that hard work, being honest, sharing my struggles, has allowed me to grow as a parent and has helped my family grow. It is okay to fail, okay to cry, okay to share, as long as we are truthful and honest in dealing with each other.

Dad's parents were early participants in the Hyde Family program, so in those days, we had yet to learn about the power of NEDs. As we review Mom and Dad's stories, we realize how much they needed help when they were students to deal with the NEDs in their families, and then help once again to deal with those NEDs when they took on the roles of parents, as well as marriage partners.

Their oldest son, Matt writes:

Growing up, I always believed when it comes to sports and basic questions, I go to my dad; when it comes to emotions, I go to my mom. I am not sure where this mindset originated from, but I had believed it unacceptable to approach my father for anything having to do with emotions.

However, now my relationship with my dad is very different. My dad would openly struggle with me and my sisters and not hide anything, making it acceptable for me to be close with him on another level. The relationship with my mom is the exact way it was when I was kid. I can talk to her about my struggles and know that she will always be there for me.

My parents had divorced when I was fifteen, then remarried three years later. During those three years, the bonds we created allowed us to stay close, even in the most desperate times. Having created this bond when I was younger allowed me to trust my sisters and I were not going to be forgotten, even though my parents were going through their own personal problems. I tried to stay out of the divorce and both my parents respected my decision.

During this time, mom and dad were honest about their own problems, allowing me to trust them and to take their advice on my own problems. Without the deep relationship we had created, I wouldn't have been able to follow their lead and become the person I am today. They showed me how to do it by being honest with me through all aspects of my life and their own.

Here we see a NED being broken. Dad told us he learned from his father to pass off problems to his wife; Matt says that growing up, when it came to emotions, "I go to my mom." But now he acknowledges his relationship with his dad is "very different;" his dad openly struggles and doesn't hide anything, allowing Matt to be close to him.

Their daughter, Susan writes:

My family, much like any other, has had a lot of struggles throughout the years. One of our biggest struggles was being overly protective of each other. My parents raised my little sister and me in a very sheltered world. I first truly noticed it the day my parents separated. The separation was a surprise to me because I did not even know they were fighting. Even though I was young, I still remember feeling I should have been able to detect something was going on.

As I grew up and matured, this sheltered lifestyle became one of our family's biggest anchors. It led me to live a life that I allowed to be planned out for me by others. I would always make sure I kept everyone happy and basically turned my back on making my own choices.

It was not until the summer before junior year at Hyde that my family truly started to become fully honest with each other. This was also the first time that I truly earned their trust. It opened up a new relationship between my parents, my siblings, and me. From that point on, it hasn't always been easy, but we certainly are still trying to keep up with the truth.

Susan reminds us that there is still a lot of work to do with the younger children, who in her words, were living "in a very sheltered world." Susan realizes she was repeating her mother's NED of trying to "keep everyone happy." But as she says, the family is "still trying to keep up with the truth," which "will set you free, but first, it will make you miserable."

As we observe Mom and Dad struggle with the NEDs in their parenting, I'm sure all of us might want to consider how well we are passing down the parent-child bonds and mentorship roles to our children.

In the next chapter, we will share how Blanche and I received these bonds from our parents, how our three children and their spouses received them from us and their parents, and then how their adult children received them. This will picture their transfer over four generations.

Chapter 9

Passing on the Bonds

At this point, we have recognized adverse childhood experiences (ACEs) as the source of our negative emotional dispositions (NEDs) and the Negative Love Syndrome, which not only cause problems in our lives, but in our children's lives as well.

We have come to understand this as the consequence of human imperfection. The more we strive in life, the more both our strengths and imperfections are revealed. And if we don't address adverse experiences, we pass them on as NEDs (along with our strengths) to the next generation.

So we need to simply view parents as unaware carriers of these NED viruses. Once they are made aware, they are in a position to develop a cure for themselves, their children, and their children's children.

My wife Blanche and I accomplished this—but without the help of what we at Hyde have learned over the past twenty-five years; we had a very difficult time. We were saved by nature's parenting power. Like the way centrifugal force makes the golf swing work, nature provides the magical connection that makes parenting work.

The Blanche-Joe Gauld Family

Both Blanche and I had our share of NEDs and the Negative Love Syndrome. (I had a score of 4 on the ACE test, and Blanche would have scored the same.)

It was only a matter of time before those NEDs threatened our connection. Alcohol was a regular part of Blanche's and my life, and while I escaped the alcoholism that hit so many in my lineage, Blanche caught the disease that was passed down in her family.

Blanche's alcoholism brought confusion into our family. I further confused things by not realizing the NED I had developed in dealing with my mother's alcoholism.

It was like I had two mothers—the sober one both my friends and I could talk to about anything, and the drunk one who might be passed out in a pool of urine or who would disappear on a three-day binge. So when my wife started drinking and changing personalities, I did everything to get her to stop drinking.

But my "help" made matters worse. By taking an active role in trying to help Blanche get sober, I unwittingly turned the focus more on me, leading to bitter arguments and separations.

Many people reject alcoholism as a disease, even though the medical profession has defined it as a disease and Alcoholics Anonymous—the most successful treatment by far—is based on this definition. Unfortunately, Blanche, as a strong and proud person, felt it was her responsibility to beat this thing, and while I intellectually understood it as a disease, emotionally my NED— my experience with my mother's alcoholism—simply focused me on her need to quit.

Little did I realize then that Blanche was not going to beat this thing with willpower, that if she hoped to find lasting sobriety, she would have to develop a profound humility that would enable her to surrender her will to a power greater than herself.

While she had automatically expressed this profound humility on the farm and then in raising her children, she stubbornly resisted doing so in her own life. She first had seen her younger brother committed to an institution for the mentally challenged, then had lost her other two brothers and her father in World War II, leaving her only her mother. Keeping a stiff upper lip regardless of circumstances had a special meaning to Blanche.

Blanche tried to beat alcoholism with her will, and I, stupidly, encouraged this losing fight by constantly telling her, "It's either me or booze." She would have stretches of sobriety, but then eventually slip and drink.

After many failures to help Blanche, I reached the final threat: divorce. Then one night my lawyer called me, "Joe, the ninety days are up. Shall I pass the papers?" I was speechless; I couldn't get my mouth to say "yes." Every move I had made was to help Blanche get sober, and now I was faced with a grim finality.

After a long pause, I said, "Buzz, I'll call you back." For the first time, I realized *I* had a problem. The NED I had developed in loyally standing by my mother's alcoholism was now repeating itself; I was determined to do whatever it took to help my wife get sober. As I put the phone down, I realized I had to attend a local Al-Anon meeting.

I had gone to Al-Anon meetings before, but just to help get Blanche sober. This was the first time I would be going to get help for myself. I explained to the group what had happened with the telephone call, that I made tough decisions every day, but this time I was speechless. When I finished, a woman at the end of the table said: "Stick around this program, and you'll be able to make that decision."

I did stick around the program, and I was eventually able to pass the papers and divorce Blanche. But we were still in contact because of the kids, and I still was trying to help her get sober. Then, five years later, I woke up and finally realized, "Joe, she's never going to quit."

My whole attitude changed. I finally let go. I deeply appreciated what Blanche had done for the kids and me, but this was her life, and I needed to let go and move on, respecting her and what she had done for all of us.

By nature, Blanche was a deeply insightful person, so I'm sure she perceived in our telephone conversations that I had let go of her. Now she no longer depended upon me or my help. Within six months she found sobriety.

As she later explained it, she couldn't accept the disease concept of alcoholism, and always felt beating the problem was a matter of willpower. It wasn't until the doctor she trusted said to her, "Blanche, if you don't quit drinking, I don't think you'll make it through the winter." She then realized she wanted to live and knew the one step she never had accepted in AA was the first—that she was powerless over alcohol, and thus she needed to turn her life over to a power greater than herself to restore her to sanity.

By taking this step, Blanche found both sobriety and serenity. It reveals the power of NEDs, and perhaps the misguided determination of both Blanche and me—she to solve her drinking problem by willpower alone, and me to encourage this. It took us fifteen years to get the help we needed.

Then, as my son Malcolm put it, "My parents declared their divorce a failure and remarried." Unfortunately, shortly before we did, we discovered that Blanche had terminal cancer. We asked her doctor how much time we had, and he said, "You'll do well to get six months."

Blanche and I were silent driving home, and then she grabbed my knee and said, "Daddy, we're going to show them how to do it." Today as I look up over my computer at her high school picture (when I first met her,) I know that she sure did. I remember the scene when she was getting a check-up and her arms were down to looking like spindles. I said, "You want to arm wrestle?" She just stuck out her tongue at me.

We had two years together, a very important time for our family. We were fortunate then that all three of our children and their spouses were working at Hyde in Bath. Laurie, Paul, and her three children lived across the street; Meddy, the youngest, said she could see Grammie Gauld from her bedroom window. Blanche was able to renew her family bonds.

Blanche had been the core of our family bond and her alcoholism and behavior had brought great confusion to the kids. They trusted the preparation for life we had developed for them; they also had to deal with times when their mother, their main model, might erupt into irrational behavior, and their father's overall approach in dealing with it proved to be ineffective.

For example, one day I announced to the kids that both Blanche and I gave up drinking. While I did quit drinking, Blanche was drunk the next day. Another day I announced to the kids that their mother was returning home from a separation because she had returned to AA with a commitment to sobriety. Within a few days she created a scene, and another separation began.

So for a family that had had a lot of integrity and stability, there was a great deal of dysfunction and distress. Fortunately, Laurie and Malcolm had reached the teen years when Blanche's alcoholic behavior really went off-track, so they were better equipped to handle it. But at eight, , Gigi was most affected. As Blanche herself said later, "I didn't do for Gigi what I did for Malcolm and Laurie."

But during those last two years, Gigi was able to make a better connection with her mother. During a Hyde seminar, she said to her, "Your getting sober was the greatest gift you ever gave me." This is a very important statement for parents to think about. Blanche was a very strong figure to her children, one they identified with. If she ultimately threw her life away in alcohol, then they believed they too probably wouldn't ultimately succeed in life. But Blanche instead left a legacy of a long struggle and many failures with an ultimate triumph. It is truly a great gift to her children.

How did our kids maintain the bond during that very confusing period when their parents, particularly their mother, the core of the family, went so far off-track? I think it's what we at Hyde call the "effort savings bank." Blanche had previously done an excellent job in leading our family, and had built a mountain of trust and respect.

So when Blanche's behavior went off-track, the kids were confused, but not cynical, and were looking for answers with positive expectations. They saw me trying, not successfully, but still not wavering. So they continued to be the same family, with Laurie becoming the mother of the house, helping to oversee Gigi. Malcolm graduated from Hyde and went to Bowdoin College in the next town during this period, so he was able to keep in close contact with the family. Blanche lived in the area, and kept in contact with the family during her sober stretches.

Trust is critical to the bond, with truth critical to trust. An episode during that time describes how it worked in our family:

I heard that Laurie was involved in a situation at the school and asked her about it. She told me what I thought was a cockamamie story, so when she finished, I looked at her in disbelief, and said, "Laurie, I don't believe you." She burst into tears and left the room. I thought, "What's wrong with you? Laurie has always played it straight with you, and the first time she tells you something that doesn't add up, you don't believe her." However the fact was, I didn't believe her. But I did trust with time, she'd tell me the truth, so I let it go and went to work on our relationship.

About a year later, we were talking about something else, and she said, "It's like that time, Dad, when you said you didn't believe me. I realized I was losing something that was very important to me that I needed to work on." So in our own ways, we both realized we needed to work on our relationship. Obviously, I now believed her story.

Except for the alcoholism, both Blanche and I maintained this level of honesty with our children. The kids always knew there was no dishonesty too small to be ignored, regardless of what it would take to deal with it. In this process, truth became a foundation of our relationships, and with it, trust, so essential to our parent-child bonds.

When Blanche and I started to have children, it was clear to me that her first concern was always what was expected out of her and me in order to raise our kids properly. This was not in any way a defensive or worried concern, but rather a matter-of-fact, what should we do now? She could be very decisive, yet very willing to accept my alternate suggestions, even on big decisions.

Blanche had a humility that allowed her to trust our parenting instincts—as if nature had given us this job to do and the abilities to do it, while we were still open to learn from the parenting we saw around us. It's not that we were oblivious to the demands of society's achievement culture, but we were first always focused on what we perceived to be the needs of our children, and I believe our children came to trust this in us.

When we were concerned that the local school wasn't challenging Malcolm in seventh grade, I arranged for several conferences with his teachers and asked them to put him in a higher track. They said they wanted him to earn it. I told them "But he's as happy as a pig in garbage running with his friends and playing ball." One teacher finally said, "Mr. Gauld, what's the problem? Mal is a good kid and he's doing fine." When I reported all this back to Blanche, she simply said, "We've got to send him away to school."

We sent Mal to a very traditional boarding school, and we were aware he was unhappy; today he calls it the unhappiest year of his life—he later described it as "perpetual embarrassment." But we also knew he was getting the challenge he needed. In June, when he was thirteen, Malcolm was given the choice to return to that school or not. I told him, "You know this is expensive for us, which your mother and I will gladly pay, but only if you make the commitment to return."

My heart was in my throat, but I was putting my trust in him and in our parent-child bond. It was reaffirming that he never hesitated in going back. While later in his life he told me troubling stories about his experiences there, the one thing that stuck out for him was, "I was in with people who were going somewhere, and I realized I was going nowhere." But it was also true he would have lost our respect if he didn't go back, and I was confident that would be unacceptable to him.

As usual, Blanche's great instincts caught Malcolm's condition at his eighth-grade graduation as he was receiving his diploma. We were in the audience and she grabbed my hand, and said, "Joey! He can't even look up!" Sure enough, Mal's head was down the entire time he walked across the stage, a testament to the state of his self-confidence.

In those days, it was thought to be a conflict to have your child attend the school where you were the headmaster, so we planned to send Mal to a school that would take him in the tenth grade. So what to do in the ninth grade? Since as headmaster I did the in-depth interviews of every family, I decided to discipline myself to conduct our family interview as a professional; I was sure I could separate myself as his father while he was at Hyde.

I was surprised at my ability to objectively conduct the interview and focus on Mal's lack of confidence. I became so immersed in his thoughts and feelings, I was stunned when Blanche got up and walked out of the interview!

It was hard for me to understand her act at the time, since I felt the interview was needed to help Mal begin to develop his self-confidence. What I did not appreciate then was that I was putting the headmaster role ahead of the more critical father role, which Blanche was protecting.

It worked out. Within the gates I was a professional; at home, I was Dad.

There are similar stories about how we handled the development of Laurie and Gigi that would give you the picture of the bonds we had with them. It is a bond that has continued since Blanche's death in 1991; our entire family—now me, the three children and their spouses, and nine grandchildren—renews this bond every year with a reunion.

*

The bonds we have formed in our respective families can be accomplished in any family. But in my work, I often encounter strained relationships, a loss of respect, broken trust, cross purposes—many dysfunctions that are interfering with what could and should be synergistic relationships between parent and child.

There is a right and natural way to parent children. It supersedes the fact that every child is different, and that all of us have a different parenting style. Once we are able to drop into this natural groove, and then discipline our parenting to stay in that groove, the flow we experience encourages both parent and child to work together in their common purpose.

King Solomon in his wisdom understood that a mother's true connection is to the child's future, not to the child. As much as a true parent loves and cares for a child, the larger concern is always: is my child learning to do his/her best? Is s/he becoming self-sufficient? Is s/he being fully prepared for life?

Now consider that children know they must have such a caretaker not only for survival, but to be prepared for life. This is the parent they really want—and need.

I asked my three children, their spouses, and my grandchildren what they consider important in their families, sending them a few paragraphs in the introduction in my book so they had an idea of my focus. However, I emphasized that I would like their independent thoughts. All wrote independent from each other.

The Malcolm and Laura Gauld Family

Malcolm writes:

I remember showing my report card to my parents in 3rd (I think) grade. The grades were good and we were talking about the checklist on the back that dealt with a range of issues from tardiness to penmanship to attentiveness. At one point I pointed to the one that read "Respect For the Rights of Others" and said, "You and Mom would be pretty upset if I ever got that check, huh?" My father replied, "Yup."

Even at that age, I knew that the character was more important than the grades. This is not to say that the grades were irrelevant, only that I and my sisters always knew that who we were mattered more than what we could do. The funny thing is that I had a stint from around 5th grade on through junior high when I am sure that my teachers and some of my friends' parents might well have doubted my parents' effectiveness. I cheated at school, stole from stores, and lied on a regular basis. It wasn't until high school that I consciously decided to put those attitudes and behaviors behind me.

I knew those things were wrong,

I also knew that I would never get back on track at school unless I stopped engaging in them. However, through it all, I somehow knew that I was going to have to extricate myself simply by being a better person and eventually began to accept the idea that being a better person was its own reward. I knew that the way I was living was at odds with the basic ethos of my home and family. I guess I just had to spend some time on the dark side before I could see the light. Thankfully, my family embodied that ethos as it gave me a target to keep in the back of my mind.

I credit my parents with establishing a fairly straightforward picture of what good character looked like. I learned a lot of it by testing the limits. When they would say, "The worst thing you can do in our family is lie," I had to see if I could successfully lie. (It wasn't lying if no one else knew, right?) I'd say that our family was a good laboratory for experimenting with our morality.

This is not to say that all was ideal. There were contra-dictions. My mother's alcoholism probably affected us in more ways than we know. (At the same time, I would bet that her recovery did the same in a positive sense.) My father's conduct on the tennis court was both embarrassing and weird to me, and probably compounded in my mind due to what I perceived to be little or no commitment to address it. Then again, I eventually came to see that my parents were people, too, with their own shortcomings to address.

The critical question is: As a parent myself, which was the stronger compulsion—the compulsion to emulate my own parents or the compulsion to differ from them? In my case, I'd vote resoundingly for the former. As they say, by the time a man realizes that his parents were right, he has kids who think he's wrong. And so it goes.

Mal makes some interesting and important points:

- Who our children were was more important than what they could do. I was raised the same way.
- We all have a dark side. Mal did well to confront his in junior high school. Later, Hyde helped him confirm his integrity. In his freshman year at Bowdoin, he was in danger of flunking chemistry, and his roommate, who had to take the final a day early, left a copy of the exam on Mal's desk. Mal tore it up. Once you experience integrity, you never want to lose it.

It pains me to remember my anger on the tennis courts. (I'm sure it's why Blanche got me a golf membership.) As Mal says, I had no commitment to address it. It's no excuse, but this was a NED my brother Tom and I internalized from our mother, who was high- spirited and quick to anger. As I look back today, I'm amazed how much anger sometimes controlled me on a tennis court—and once in a while, when my golf swing went south. It meant a great deal to me that Mal enrolled in a great program to address this NED I passed on to him, and that I did, too.

Laura writes:

My family of origin is a mix of both wonderful memories and tough ones as well. When I was three, my father died in a car accident. While I only had two very vague memories of him, his absence remained with me throughout my childhood. My mother did the best she could to make all of us three girls feel loved, but of course, our best intentions are never perfect. I do distinctly remember my mother making me feel like I "could do anything" I set my mind to.

Years later, my mother married my stepfather, who was a disciplinarian and not interested in friendship. At first, we all thought we "hated" him, but as the years went on, we grew to love him and appreciated what he taught us: hard work, "never say can't," girls can do anything a boy can, do a job well, etc. In fact, his infamous line was"In life, you will only compete with ten percent of the people, because ninety percent will not do the necessary work." When he died several years ago, we were all there, and I was filled with gratitude for what he gave me.

My husband Malcolm and I have been married over thirty years. We were married young and did not have our first child until we had been together for eleven years. We had both been through challenges in the marriage, and we were ready to be parents. We also were drawn together because of our principles as well as our attraction for each other. Therefore, we certainly had struggles as parents, but we have never been too far apart on the "big things," which in our family meant honesty, courage, responsibility, hard work, and integrity. At this point, our oldest is still in college. We are proud of all of them, yet I suspect the real test as to how well we did will be the kind of adults they become. (I hope to see it in my lifetime!)

One of our children has autism and that single obstacle shaped the core of our family and helped turn all of our obstacles into opportunities. As a parent, I have learned that in the challenges, I find my best self. Malcolm and I have been blessed to have three children and an extended family of committed individuals to help us in the parenting process. When you let go of having a bond and then focus on your parenting, you eventually find a connection to your child that inspires your next phase in life.

Families who raise an autistic child either seem to get consumed by the process, or become better people, like this family. I just wish Harrison, my grandchild with autism, had the skills to participate in this book. He is now seventeen, and is just now going away to school—like his two older sisters in college. He and I have played our special game (where, after I play a monster, he leads me in a repetitious conversation)almost daily since he was eight years old, and I have been his most affectionate and best friend.

I think Laura developed a NED in response to her stepfather's very heavy hand in parenting, which led her to consciously avoid that with her kids, and perhaps why her daughter, Mahalia, was sometimes called "Manipuhalia." But trust and mutual respect keeps the bond in place.

Their daughter Mahalia writes:

The bonds in my family went through a long process of growth; one that I think is still evolving. Now that I am older, I have really come to appreciate the bond I share with both my parents. When I was younger, I had a lot of resentments toward them. I felt they had to act a certain way because of their jobs and positions within our small community.

As we have gone through many experiences, I now recognize what they were trying to achieve. I feel comfortable going to them for support, guidance, advice, and just an ear to listen.

I also know I will hear the hard truths from them, even if I initially disagree. While the bond with both my mother and father is somewhat different, both bonds are based on the same values that we uphold as a family. Integrity, leadership, and honesty are words that come to mind.

Reading the introduction [to this book] gave me insight on the journey my parents and I have gone through, especially when it mentioned, "when children do not accept the direction of their parents, the bond is not formed."

For so long I wanted to fight the bond, simply just to rebel. Once I realized that neither of us could control the bond is when it flourished. I came to understand that I was the one who wanted a real connection to both parents and wanted to work on that relationship. I am so grateful for the opportunities and support they have provided me, and I value the leadership that I feel I will practice when I have my own children.

Their daughter "Scout" writes:

I think my family has never strayed from a key principle: Truth over Harmony. Sometimes Mahalia and I got lost in our lies when we were younger, but despite our slip-ups, my parents had a way of always encouraging us to be honest.

I've known other parents who took enabling roles to shield themselves from witnessing the issues their children were experiencing; for example, not bringing up touchy subjects like substance abuse, relationships with the opposite sex, expectations at school, etc. But I felt my mother in particular pioneered through the awkwardness and created a forum where I felt comfortable talking about those more difficult topics.

It isn't easy being honest with your parents when you've done something you know they disapprove of. Despite this, my parents never let the hard conversations go, and they continued to push my siblings and me towards conversations where it was freeing to be honest and have the opportunity to talk to them. I feel many children don't utilize "just talking" with their parents. Young adults neglect to realize our parents experienced many of the things we are struggling with.

Looking back on my childhood, being grounded by my parents and having to endure their disappointment in the moment was not fun and sometimes made me not like them. But once I was older it allowed me to see they always had my best interests at heart. So I felt more comfortable reaching out to them when I was confronted with problems, whether it was self-confidence issues, peer pressure, or relationship issues.

In my young adult life, I've already met a number of people my age who don't feel comfortable talking with their parents about tough, awkward issues. This makes me sad. I know my parents (and entire family for that matter) will never hesitate to support me when I need their endorsement or to challenge me on decisions they feel do not represent my character. They will also trust in my final decision. All of our strengths and challenges are a work in progress and are continually being tested, but our commitment as a family to never stop working on them is what sets us apart and helps us grow.

The Gigi and Don MacMillan Family

Don writes:

I believe for both my family of origin and my family now, the "bond" probably began in the marriage. We as future parents had the same or at least similar ideas about the importance of raising children as well as shared values in raising children. In both families, raising kids was and is of central importance; egos would have to be set aside and teamwork would be essential. Not that we knew how to do it or even did it well all the time, but we knew we couldn't mess with parenting.

Once the kids came, I think a lot of the trust came from disciplining them, meaning, when they needed correction, they got it. This will sound too familiar, but my parents, and I think Gigi and I, did not need our kid's love, nor did we worry too much about them liking us. In fact, there were times I went out of my way to make life a little difficult for the kids because I believed it would serve them better in the future.

On the kids' side, both Kayla and Hannah have told me at different times that even when they were arguing with me (as they did getting into their teen years), they were always listening and thinking about what I had told them. That enabled me to relax a little while still giving them direction, knowing they needed and wanted it.

Other keys—apologizing to the kids when we were wrong. I think this helped them understand what part of our relationship was personal and what part wasn't. Talking to them after correcting them—sounds like a no-brainer, but especially when they were young, we'd discipline them and then talk about why it had happened and asked for their input or thoughts. I believe we even did this when they were real young. I think it let them know that it wasn't "personal" when they got disciplined, and it set us up as people they could talk to even when they did something wrong.

Lastly, the kids saw Gigi and me talk and disagree—we didn't hide much, except when it was obviously more than a young kid should hear. I think they saw that it was part of being in a family to work things out.

In my family growing up, I can remember distinctly my parents sitting at the kitchen table and talking about problems and themselves after my father got sober—a very big change from before. I guess it stuck in my mind that part of getting better and being happier was sitting at the table and talking and not running from life's situations. I could trust my parents because I knew they had faced their problems head on, and so they wouldn't judge me.

It is clear Don was raised in a family much like Gigi's. In fact both Don and Gigi were working at Hyde and happened to be working together on a student camping trip when Gigi ended up telling Don what she really thought of him. The story goes that that's when Don realized he wanted to marry this girl who was going to be that honest with him.

Gigi's story:

Like many people, I remember saying, "I'll never do that when I have kids!" I was determined to raise my children differently. I wanted to be close to my children, and most importantly, be there for them in a way my mother was not there for me due to her struggle with alcoholism.

But I was fortunate to marry a man whose objective was not that type of relationship with our children, but rather preparing them for life. These two different objectives led to some conflict between us because he was often the "bad guy" with me the "good guy." My idea of being there for my kids was often criticized by my husband as babying them. But we were both very much in sync when it came to demanding respect, integrity, doing the right thing, and accountability.

As teenagers, our children attended Hyde School where both my husband and I worked. I began to learn how to parent more effectively. My first lesson was to stop doing for my children what they were capable of doing for themselves.

I remember my oldest daughter coming into my office in tears because she had failed a Spanish test. As she rather dramatically expressed her frustration and blamed the teacher, I was listening, but off to the races in my head, plotting how to solve the problem, and what to say to the teacher!

But suddenly I realized she was not asking me to do that. In fact, she was not asking me for anything. So I kept my mouth shut and continued to listen. When she finished, I responded by saying, "Sounds like you are having a tough day; is there anything I can do to help?" She said, "No!" and stomped out of my office.

I wanted to run after her, hug her, tell her it was going to be all right and we would figure it out, but I knew that would send the wrong message because she was capable of handling this situation herself. A week later she came home for dinner on Mother's Day. I was about to serve dessert when she abruptly got up from the table and announced she had to go back to campus because she had a meeting with her Spanish teacher. I calmly said "Oh, okay," but inside I was thinking "Yes!! This approach really works!"

I began to see that my parenting was too much about me. Unintentionally, it was as if I was trying to make up for what I didn't receive from my parents growing up. I needed to be more focused on what my children needed to learn in order to be prepared for life. I didn't realize how much my best intentions were undermining my children's self-confidence.

I have adopted some mantras that I have learned along the way to help me stay on track in my parenting, which are:

- *Don't do anything for your kids that they can for themselves*
- *Be the parent your kids need you to be, not the parent you want to be*
- *Be less of a manager and more of a consultant*

I am beginning to see some of the results of our parenting. When issues surface in their lives that they are not sure how to handle, they seek our guidance or use us as a sounding board. I am still careful not to offer advice unless asked! I'm very grateful for changing my priorities. I actually have the kind of relationship I always hoped I would have.

Gigi's NED from her mother's alcoholism started her parenting off on the wrong foot; her husband helped her balance it. Interestingly, Don had a similar NED from his father. Eight years after his Dad had found sobriety, Don went to father and told him he still carried resentments regarding his drinking. His dad, who then managed an alcoholic recovery organization, advised him to go to Al-Anon. His wisdom not only pointed his son in the right direction for help, but ended up helping Gigi's parenting as well.

To help readers understand this, the son's problem was emotional dispositions he had developed in dealing with his dad's alcoholism that still troubled him. The father had had a different problem: alcohol, and thus couldn't help him. But the son could go to Al-Anon where he could share his problem with others who had gone through the same experience he had and share what they had learned in their recovery.

By getting this help, Don didn't carry this NED into his parenting. So it helped set a better standard for their kids to rely upon, which, as we noted in Gigi's story, helped her expect Kayla to deal with her problems in Spanish class.

Their oldest daughter Kayla writes:

My brother and sister have had different experiences and situations with their personal relationships with my parents; each one of us does have our own bond with our parents that developed in our own ways, which I think is very unique to our family. When I read your description on the child-parent relationship, I instantly thought it related to my relationship with each of my parents; however, reaching that place with each of my parents was a different journey. My mom and I connected very early on in my life. She did not have the best relationship with her mother, Blanche. As I got older, mom became a bigger influence in my life, constantly telling me she wanted me to be able to come and talk to her if I ever was in trouble or needed her. She told me she didn't feel comfortable going to her mother when she needed something or had questions and never wanted us to feel that way.

Mom had a very good handle on the friend/mother balance, which I always really appreciated. I also think the deep bond with my mother began when we started struggling with the same things at the same time. After I began at Hyde, I realized how unhappy I was with my weight and just how low my self-confidence was, and thus began my struggle with my physical appearance.

However, my mom has also struggled with the same thing, and knowing that I wasn't alone and having such a committed role model to look up to in this particular field was always so comforting. But also knowing she was going to really push me led me to respect her so much as a mother, friend, and role model. My relationship with my father has mostly been a struggle, and our deep connection didn't come to pass until recently. The biggest struggle between my father and me was a feeling of constant misunderstanding. He found me to be over-dramatic and constantly on defense, while I found him to be insensitive and unwilling to listen to me. While we made strides forward, it wasn't until two years ago that I really felt that deep bond between us.

I started realizing that all the times he was hard on me and trying to teach me various lessons that I hated learning began coming into play more and more in my life as I got older. I realized that while I thought my father was not understanding me and being "insensitive," actually he was being tough on me so that I would learn lessons he knew were important to learn. The older I get and the more I see this factor in play, the more I realize my father and I shared that deep bond long before I felt or realized it.

My parents play two different roles in my life and the path to those deep bonds I share with both of them took different directions, but the destination I've found is the same. When our family is struggling, we sit down and discuss it, however long that takes. That is how my parents have always dealt with their disagreements together, and in front of us. Therefore, teaching my siblings and me to talk amongst each other in dealing with our disagreements has led us to be a functional family unit.

We may note that Gigi's NED with her mother, which led her to seek a close relationship with Kayla, initially encouraged a "nice parent-tough parent" dichotomy between herself and Don, making her parenting less effective, and Don's job tougher. But once she addresses this NED, both parents were strengthened.

Their younger daughter Hannah writes:

When my bond with my parents was weaker, I think fear induced my hesitation to connect with them. I was afraid of letting my parents into my life and afraid of opening up lines of communication. I wanted to keep my emotions and thoughts to myself because I didn't want my parents to judge me or get angry at the things I told them. My parents never stopped trying to talk to me, and even if I wouldn't open they would tell me they were always there for me. Although it seems elementary now, I found my parents weren't against me, and they never will be. Once I accepted their bond with me was not an attempt to destroy me, I was able to utilize their wisdom and their help.

I have really come to appreciate the bond I have with my parents. I feel I can go to them for help and guidance whenever I need it. I am comfortable enough to admit to failures and shortcomings and ask for their advice on how to move forward. The bond I have with my parents has not always been so open, however, and during my younger teen years I resisted this bond through whatever means.

If I had read the introduction describing the parent-child bond prior to reconciling with my own parents, I would not have understood the concept of such a bond. Reading it now that my parents and I are closer, I recognize each of the aspects that describe such a relationship.

It seems amazing that Hannah had those fears about her parents when she was younger. She was always an outstanding student, model citizen and excellent athlete—just like her father was. I suspect it was a NED she internalized from her father, who once told me that growing up, he fought with his dominant twin almost every day. She certainly has opened up now.

The Laurie and Paul Hurd Family

Laurie and her husband Paul's three children have all graduated from college and are now pursuing their respective careers. Here are the responses of their family.

Laurie writes:

Paul and I married each other with the intention to help nurture the other's unique potential. Our love for each other is grounded in this intention. Having children was an extension of this, too. We believed that our kids each had a unique purpose and we had been "tapped" to guide it along until they were ready to assume that responsibility for themselves. We were all accountable to each other, but more importantly, we were accountable to this belief that we were caretakers of something special within us. This belief created the bond among us.

Our bond was made up of a belief in each other and in something beyond us (a higher purpose), trust, humor, and an effort to stay connected. We had people in our lives that helped us stay true to our bond, too. They helped us ask tough questions when we needed it and sometimes when we didn't need it.

We took time to evaluate the bond and how well we were doing as parents; not just our own assessment, but from people who knew us, as well as from people who didn't know us. It was hard to go through those questions and examinations but it was essential for our perspective. Paul and I also looked at our own lives and how we were doing in developing our potentials. It was like keeping several plates in the air and spinning at once.

We were fortunate to have a process that helped provide a map for parenting, with other people to help us. Our kids didn't always like our decisions. As a matter of fact, they were angry and resentful about some decisions, and that tested the bond.

We've worked at creating a new bond now that they are adults and in charge of their own lives. It's a continuing relationship that works on honesty, trust, and humor. These are some of my thoughts. It's a bond that is a constant work in progress.

This is what sticks out to me about Laurie's thoughts:

- Her family emphasis on unique potential repeats Malcolm's comment regarding who you are being more important than what you can do, and takes that form because everyone had a Hyde education that was built on the premise *"Every individual is gifted with a unique potential that defines a destiny."*
- Laurie and Paul guided their family by basic principles and utilized the Hyde community of teachers and families to help them stay true to their principles, even when their kids didn't like their decisions.

- I think Laurie's NED came more from becoming the mother in our house once her mom's alcoholism took over, and so led her to take her job so seriously that sometimes she doubted herself.
- They are now in a new relationship with their adult children that utilizes honesty, trust, and humor to continue the bond.

Here are Paul's remarks (Paul was the first student I interviewed for Hyde in 1966):

Our family bond generates from a deep belief in another's mutual commitment to the truth; a belief that each of us is gifted with a unique potential (that everyone else in the family must honor); an abiding love for one another's foibles and frustrations; and an encompassing sense of humor that allows no one to take themselves too seriously.

As parents, we have been blessed with two sets of grandparents who believed in our kids the same way that we did and astounded all of us in the nuclear family with their sense of compassion and depth of sacrifice for our children. We were gifted with an extended family whose love always came through as both challenging and supportive. Our many sponsored gatherings and vacations together always offered fun as well as reflection. Though we were all working at similar goals with our respective nuclear families, it was very important to compare variations on the theme of forging that bond.

We also had a great school (which all of us were fortunate enough to attend as students). It functioned as a major catalyst for our ongoing growth as individuals and as a family unit. It put emphasis upon working through mistakes and always searching to improve how well we could work together.

Through our children we also met many other parents and families who were trying to develop a similar kind of bond of respect and growth. These parents and kids taught us much about respecting other and new perspectives on growth, as well as more about respecting one another. Athletic contests and performing arts shows offered many opportunities to listen as well as to share differing approaches to our respective ties.

Our three children continue to deepen our bond as they grow older and find that directives from their parents have given way to more peer-like discussions. In many ways the original motivation for the bond in our family has reversed for me personally, and I find I am more the learner from my children's love and wisdom.

Articulating the bond itself seems difficult because its development required such diverse constituencies and efforts. Perhaps it is best captured in our original family mission statement: "Led by conscience; strengthened by mistakes; bound by humor." We have all been learners with one another, and the patience and belief that has constituted is love.

Several Points:

- Paul was raised by exceptionally fine people who were humble to a fault. This led to a NED of self-confidence that took Paul some years to fully overcome.
- Note the emphasis on family principles, which Paul later articulates in the family mission statement: "Led by conscience; strengthened by mistakes; bound by humor."
- Paul also mentions the traditional support system of the family—grandparents, extended family, peer group, school community. This is one of the great strengths that all Hyde families have.
- Paul also notes the changing relationship with his children, where they are all learning from each other.

Their son Zach writes:

*At a very early age my parents made it pretty clear
that "truth" was going to be our family's foundation. In
order for us to have strong, meaningful relationships
with each other, we had to be honest with each other.
Although I followed this rule (with some snags along the
way) it felt more due to fear of some sort of punishment.
As time went on, this idea of "truth" really started to
change. My dad had always been the authoritarian in our
household. In my younger years, it felt like he was more
focused on enforcing rules than being someone I felt comfortable approaching. However, in my teens, our relationship
began to deepen. He began opening up to me about his fears,
hopes, and aspirations. I saw him more clearly as a human
being and someone I could really ... trust. Watching him and
my mother openly struggle and work through difficulties in
their relationship started to give me the understanding that
these were people that were practicing what they were asking
of my sisters and me.*

*Dad making himself vulnerable to me gave me confi-
dence he was always going to give me a fair assessment of
what he thought. Dad could always be my friend, but this
didn't necessarily make me see him as a mentor I wanted
to approach. When I really saw the deeper sides of him,
that's when I felt like this was someone that I wanted
to consult when I needed guidance. I still feel this way
today, which is why I usually find myself calling my parents when I'm in the midst of making a difficult decision.*

I think several points should be highlighted here:

- We must first establish a role of authority with our children (like the amusing teaching adage: "Don't smile until
Christmas.") Zach is at first in fear of the emphasis on truth

and the authoritarian atmosphere. But once it is accepted, he is able to be more open with his father.

- However, it is interesting that it is not the friendship with his father that leads him to accept his father as a mentor. It is how the authoritarian shows his "deeper sides."

Oldest daughter Georgia writes:

There was nothing ordinary about growing up in the Hurd family. I looked around at my classmates in elementary school and saw my parents operated on a completely different level when it came to childrearing. There was no nightly family dinner at six o'clock or school lunches and outfits our mother put together; we were participants in the living, breathing organism of Hyde School. My parents were fiercely committed to their work at the school, which pushed us kids to embrace independence and responsibility.

My family relationships continue to be the most important connections I have in my life today. I felt my parents support and push from a young age, with a serious investment in my growth academically and athletically as well as creatively. They pushed me to play sports even when I refused to get out of the car for soccer practice and hired tutors when they saw me struggle in math. My stubbornness was matched consistently with my parents' challenge to push through what scared me most; I could not hide! I remember feeling bogged down by the pressures of school and high expectations most of my life. I made up excuses and lied to get out of anything that might expose my weaknesses. I pushed my family away, but they refused to stay locked out. My family has seen me through dark times and never once let me take the easy way out. Their strength and belief in me helped me get through a difficult period in my life. These people see me for who I truly am, and it's terrifying and empowering all at the same time. We

*can laugh with one another but also be brutally honest.
What's most amazing to me is how our bond has grown,
changed, and strengthened throughout the years. Today, I live
on the other side of the country, what feels to be a world apart
from my family, but I feel closer to them now than I've ever
felt. At the core of our family bond is a deep respect for the
truth, unique potential, and the ability to laugh at ourselves.*

Georgia talks about her stubbornness being met by her parent's
challenge to push through what scared her the most; then her
family seeing her for who she truly is, which was terrifying and
empowering at the same time. Now she has the courage to pursue
being an actress in Hollywood!

Daughter Meddy writes:

*Growing up, I always asked my parents "why can't we be like nor-
mal families?" Normal to me meant comfort. It meant not uproot-
ing every two years. It meant not being forced to participate in
family mandatory fun. [note: a Hyde term for a required family
fun activity] It meant not having to discuss uncomfortable topics on a regular basis. Normal meant harmony.*

*From a young age I felt a sense of respect and loyalty toward
my parents. My family, for the most part, always got along, and
we enjoyed spending time together. However, I resented my parents' intentional intrusion [note: a Hyde term for helping someone else, even when they don't ask for help], and I resented their
ability to step back and allow me to struggle on my own.*

*I envied my friends' disconnected relationships with
their parents, which looked convenient and comfortable. In
my family, truth and honesty were always most important.
Morals and values were never to be compromised even if
it jeopardized our harmony. My parents were committed to my
potential, beyond whatever I thought I was capable of.*

In college I began to see my discontent and fear of failure was not solely tied to the fear of my parents' disappointment. I had begun to develop my own standards and my own confidence. I was no longer willing to settle for less than what I felt I was capable of.

My parents have now modeled a way that my entire family interacts together. We have always been expected to act from a place of conscience with one another; that is not an option but an obligation. The bond I feel with my parents allows me to hear their concern from a deep genuine place that is tied to the person I want to become. That is someone unique and thriving.

Like her brother and sister, Meddy honors her spirit and initially challenges or questions the unique family bond, and like them, comes to appreciate its strength. It might indicate their character development that all three were chosen to captain their college lacrosse teams.

We need to appreciate that kids have spirit, and that it is natural for them to test limits and even rebel against the standards we set for them. We saw Malcolm report that he lied, cheated, and stole from the fifth through the eighth grade when he knew telling the truth was the most important value in our family. But since then he has gained wide respect as a man of integrity. As he explained, he felt his family essentially challenged him to find out if he could successfully lie; at some point, he realized that was not the life he wanted for himself, and not just because we told him it was wrong.

We see Meddy taking a similar path. First, "Why can't we be normal like other families?" Then-"I envied my friends disconnected relationships with their parents." This is really not a girl rebelling against her parents, it is a girl trying to respect her own spirit.

When Blanche and I married the second time, Laurie's family had their picture taken. Meddy had her back to camera, refusing to face the camera.

I love that picture. Meddy was about four years old at the time. Here is this little kid saying, "Look, you can't push me around; I'm someone you have to reckon with!" It's an attitude where she is overstepping herself, and now she will have to begin to learn the meaning of humility. But she is taking an important step in standing up for herself, no matter how amusing the setting.

I believe if kids do not experience the act of standing up for themselves in childhood, it is unlikely that they will stand up for themselves in life.

I think it is important to note that all three of these families raised spirited kids who challenged their parenting, and it was in their parents' holding to their principles and what they believed to be right—while still listening to their kids—that they gained their respect, trust and love in order to become their mentors.

I think Mahalia speaks for all my grandchildren when she says, "I value the leadership that I feel I will practice when I have my own children."

As we step back and think about the stories of transformation of the parents in the last three chapters, we can see the commonality of stories.

We were all raised by parents who had a sense of purpose in life, and who raised us in that sense, and to be the best we could be.

But our parents were not taught how to love without negative emotional dispositions, and thus were unable to teach us how to love without negative emotional dispositions. Since love is essential to human feelings of self worth, this resulted in negative patterns for them, which we internalized from them.

Thanks to the help that all of us received from Hyde, and some of us from Hoffman, we all were able to begin the process of transcending these negative patterns and emphasize the strengths we gained from our parents, together with spirit, unique potentials, and capacity to love.

Chapter 10

Final Steps

Recognizing the difficulties of trying to raise children as a single parent, perhaps the single most important decision in raising children is whom we choose for a spouse. The American divorce rate that is over fifty percent does not signify a healthy atmosphere for raising children.

I'm pleased to say a number of Hyde graduates marry each other. While we don't have statistics, they rarely seem to divorce and do seem to form bonded families. They obviously share the same values and a common sense of purpose, which I believe is the foundation for both successful marriages and successful families.

This was certainly true for Blanche and me. Not only did my family share the same values and sense of purpose with Blanche's family, but Blanche and I share the same values and sense of purpose with the families of the spouses of our children.

As some examples of this:

When Laurie's husband Paul was a student at Hyde, I had to discipline him for allowing some classmates to copy his French homework. Paul's father called me, "We understand the seriousness of the situation, and wondered if it will be necessary for Paul to leave Hyde."

Malcolm's Laura lost her father in automobile accident and was raised by a stepfather as strict as mine. But like mine, he was committed to help the children become all they were meant to be, as noted in how he parented Laura when she took the family car without permission at age 15

I wrote about how Gigi's husband Don went to his father and told him he had a problem with his dad's drinking, eight years after his dad had been sober, and how his dad, instead of accepting the responsibility, which would have simply continued Don's NED, wisely directly Don to Al-Anon.

All three of these families have dedicated mothers, which is why fathers like us were able to have the influence we have had. Together with our wives, we agreed on a foundation of values and principles, and with this in place, it was easy to come to agreements on how best to raise our kids, because we all recognized we were rookies at it, accepting whatever help we could get, but beginning with our own families, not with our families of origin.

Parents who disagree over how to raise children are either at odds over values or have preconceived ideas on how children should be raised because of their own childhood experience. In either case, it is a losing argument for the kids, because the parents are not on the same page.

Back to Basics: Nature's Bond

So at this point, let us take an inventory once more of what we need to do to establish the parent-child bond so our children will accept us as mentors. No matter what our present relationship is with our child, it is possible to establish all of these conditions, which will create the bond and fully create us as our children's mentors.

1. Commitment to Our Best
We have a commitment to ensure that both we and our children always do our best and give our best effort in any endeavor. We

> **Our highest respect is always reserved for our best effort, regardless of the outcome.**

maintain a continual quest for excellence. While we take pleasure in our achievements, our highest respect is always reserved for our best effort, regardless of the outcome. We know our best draws out our unique potential, which leads us on the path of our destiny.

Since we live in an achievement culture where the emphasis is overwhelmingly on our children's academic prowess, we must emphasize our commitment to our children's best and their unique potential.

We take care to make sure our children know this commitment is at the foundation of our relationship with them, and that we will let nothing interfere with it. We make sure they know our expectations of them will always be based on our deeper belief in the best in them. This helps them to develop confidence in what they can do, as well as an acceptance of what they cannot do.

Helping our children realize their best is a major task that requires patience. For example, we need to play more the role of a teacher and not take our children's progress or reaction to our mentoring personally. We see in them what they don't yet see in themselves.

Since we are not perfect, we need to share our own shortcomings in reaching our own best with our children. We also have to prioritize areas of importance in challenging our kids. For example, we may decide to cut Junior some slack in some area because of the other expectations we are placing on him.

2. Prepare Children for Self-Sufficiency

We have to prepare our children to be able to take the major responsibility for their lives by roughly age nineteen. While most of the critical work for self-sufficiency happens in adolescence, we need to begin in childhood by giving our children household chores and then encourage their individual enterprises like lemonade stands, paper routes, rocketry, etc.

Adolescence should emphasize challenge and risk, so we parents have to ease up on our protection of our teenagers. They need to struggle with the rigors of academics, athletics, peer pressure, and the search for their identities. We can *play a powerful mentoring role in this period by largely staying out of the struggle*,

We need to share our own shortcomings.

and by reassuring them that the struggle is necessary, sometimes giving some encouragement, and on very rare occasions, maybe even some advice.

We need to understand the logic: "Your children are not your children." Nature has given children to us on a lend-lease basis. We are to rigorously prepare them for life until age nineteen or so, and then let them go. If we do it right, they will come back to us of their own volition. If we haven't prepared them by then, we need to develop a plan to do it as soon as we can.

3. Mentor Children to Deal with Essential Questions

In addition to helping children realize their best and become self-sufficient, we must *ensure they are prepared for life*. This is centered on helping them answer the three basic questions: Who am I? Where am I going? What do I need to get there?

Our children are seeking to imitate us from birth. In addition, our achievement-oriented society often puts pressure upon our children to "fit in," which can lead them to become someone they are not. So, as parents, we must take great care to help our children gain confidence in their own uniqueness.

If we are doing this at home, it will strengthen our children's individuality in society. However, to do this, we need to be sure to *praise their hard work, not their abilities,* as Dr. Carol Dweck of Stanford University has so clearly proven.

Dweck conducted an experiment with two groups of students. One group was praised for their intelligence and the second praised for their effort and hard work. After a series of six challenges involving both success and failure, the group praised for their intelligence was more likely to perform poorly or give up after a failure, to misrepresent how well they did on a test, to view their failures as evidence of lower intelligence, and to feel pressure and less pleasure from their work.

However, those praised for their hard work tended to see each challenge as a learning experience and a chance to show their effort, to see failure as simply a need for more effort, and to gain pleasure from the learning.

We need to teach our children to value hard work, while appreciating their efforts, whatever they may be. In this process, we hope to draw out the potentials of our children, on one hand, challenging them in ways that will ultimately contribute to helping them express their unique potential, and on the other hand, supporting them in their own efforts of self-discovery.

To ensure that our children are prepared for life, we must thoughtfully develop their character. There are many qualities of character, but Hyde parents and students have found that five Hyde qualities have proven to provide a character foundation for life.

These qualities have held up for over several generations now, so we know them now as The Pathway to Excellence:

- Curiosity: *I am responsible for my learning.*
- Courage: *I learn the most about myself through challenges and taking risks,*
- Concern: *I need a challenging and supportive community to develop my character.*
- Leadership: *I am a leader by asking the best of myself and others.*

- Integrity: *I am gifted with a unique potential. Conscience is my guide in developing it.*

The developmental sequence is: we take responsibility for our learning; we challenge ourselves; we seek a community to help us do this; we then help others do this; we ultimately learn to do the right thing. It is very powerful in its simplicity.

4. Share Our Struggles with Our Children

The fourth condition in developing our parent-child bond involves our NEDs, and sharing our efforts to deal with them with our children. This work creates the degree of excellence we hope to achieve in our parenting and in both our and our children's lives. Fulfilling the first three conditions define good and right parenting. But for families of high expectations, where excellence is a concept deep within our soul, we may find it essential to fulfill this condition, perhaps even to be successful as a parent.

I had discussed earlier that the higher our expectations in life, the more struggles and problems we will have, and thus the more NEDs we will develop, along with greater PEDs. You don't get something for nothing in life. So children of parents who fit this description will internalize some very strong qualities from the parent, but in this process, also internalize the parent's negative emotional dispositions as well.

I hope you will do with the following exercises by first applying them to yourself and then sharing the exercise with your spouse (or at least with some one you trust) and then finally sharing them with your teenage children.

In addition, it would be extremely meaningful if you would also share with your spouse and family what it was like growing up with your parents, and the positive and negative feelings you had toward them. Remember, those feelings really express the NEDs and PEDs in your family.

Dealing with Anger As a NED

If the parent doesn't recognize these NEDs and at least acknowledge them to their children, then they become qualities that undermine the best in the children, and diminish their pride in their parent and family. Children may come to resent these qualities in the parent, as well as in themselves. The parent may dislike these qualities as well. Since the family is striving for excellence, the conflicts these NEDs can cause can overwhelm the high expectations of the family.

For example, say a father has anger issues, which he internalized from his father. It costs him a job early in his career, so he learns to mute it at work, but doesn't mute it at home. His son however, in imitating his father, has anger problems in school and elsewhere. He comes to feel that's just who he is, and accepts the patterns of upset it causes in his life. His father can't identify with his son's anger, because he sees it as uncontrollable, while he has learned to control his own anger, at least at work.

Both are living lives controlled by a NED created in previous generations. If the father could recognize this, share with his son what it was like being raised by an angry father, go on to explain how he lost his job because of his anger and what he did to modify it, he would be taking the first step to pull the anger NED out of both himself and his son so that they both could look at it and begin to discuss it as an unwanted problem they share—like a virus.

They could begin to view it as a virus that entered them shortly after they both were born, and grew in them as they grew. However, their acknowledgment of it, working together on it, laughing when they realize they allow it to take control of them, are all important steps in their recovery. It was learned; it can be unlearned.

This sharing may be difficult, but it is vital in establishing our deep family bonds and our mentorship.

But even more than this, if you are unable to share your childhood with depth and "coherence," research in psychology would say there is a strong possibility you are having difficulties in parenting your children!

To summarize the research leading to this conclusion:

- There is a direct connection between a parent's childhood and his/her parenting.
- While a "secure" childhood often leads to secure parenting and "insecure" childhood to insecure parenting, that isn't the major factor.
- The major factor is not how dysfunctional or how many problems your family had. The major factor was how much parents can make real <u>sense</u> out of their childhood—a "coherence." This coherence is not just based on the logic and linguistics of their left brain, but more on the richer emotional and holistic understanding involving their right brain.

The left brain, ultimately responsible for logic, analysis, and objectivity, doesn't even kick in until age two, and kids are generally right-brain people —that's why they read our hearts, not our minds. So if you're a strong left-brain/weak right-brain parent, you'll have trouble communicating with your kids.

However, for those who were exposed to some combination of qualities like openness, challenge, depth, and structure in a childhood that was insecure because of problems and traumas, it is likely that as parents they actually had a "coherent" childhood that makes sense to them regardless of the turmoil; thus—insecure childhood, but secure parenting.

Conversely, as we have seen at Hyde, some parents profess to have had "perfect parents," but with only left-brain memories of their childhoods. Thus they haven't made good right-brain connections with their children, are emotionally unavailable and don't understand why their kids are off-track. Thus—supposedly secure childhood; but insecure parenting.

In general, my experience in helping parents talk about their childhood and their relationship with their parents confirms what psychology tells us, that those who find little to talk about in their childhood, or go on endlessly, or get lost in what they are trying to say, or become defensive, etc., generally reflect insecure parenting. But once we are able to help them open up and became more "coherent," their relationship with their children begins to improve.

I'm not saying this to hurt parents who feel dismissive, disorganized, or ambivalent about their childhood. I'm simply saying these exercises could be the first step to helping all parents become more "coherent" with their childhoods and their parents, which in turn, can further unite their families, their bonds, and mentorships.

Categories and NEDs

We all have NEDs, some more powerful in us than others, but all of us have some to some degree. No parent is perfect. As you think back to your own upbringing, here is a list of categories that might help stimulate your thinking about possible NEDs you internalized and passed on to your children.

I suggest you write down on a separate piece of paper those words that might fit some of the negative attitudes, behaviors, moods or patterns of both you and/or your parents. (You might mark "I" for you, "M" for mother "F" for father, and "SM" and "SF" for stepparents.)

Remember, identifying their negative patterns does not say you didn't have great parents! But no matter how good they were, they were raised by imperfect parents, so through no fault of their own, they did internalize negative emotional dispositions and the Negative Love Syndrome.

Categories

1. Unloving, unavailable, or uncaring
Abandoned, neglected, unprotected, sent away, rarely home, undemonstrative, rarely showed affection or said "I love you," few close relationships, detached, withdrawn, indifferent, depressed.

2. Careless or distracted
False promises, unpredictable or moody, neglectful, lies, forgetful, thoughtless or careless, unreliable, created a crisis, frequently late, postponed important tasks, made excuses, indulgent, bad with money, gambling.

3. Submissive or subservient
Passive, self-doubt, lack of confidence, resigned, jealous, puts self down, defensive, martyr, self-pity, easily hurt, self-sacrificing, disappointed, made others feel guilty, shame.

4. Fear and anxiety
Exaggerated dangers, anticipated the worst, expected failure or rejection, apprehensive or nervous, always in a hurry, tense, worrier, phobias, fear of the unknown, lived in the past, fear of not doing it right, afraid to disappoint anyone, afraid to be alone.

5. Image-conscious and love seeker
Show off, notice me, social climber and status seeker, need to be special, superficial, need to impress others, narcissistic, need to be right, above all be charming, condescending, overly friendly, difficult to say "no," always doing for others.

6. Critical
Fault finder, blames self or others, prejudiced, intolerant, self-loathing, superior, perfectionist, unrealistic expectations, never good enough, driven, never satisfied.

7. **Invalidates:**
   Authority, self, feelings, love, spirituality, children or spouse, career, happiness, fun, change or dreams.

8. **Controlling or rigid**
   Dominating, stubborn, denial, inflexible, stern, intimidating, strict disciplinarian, abusing power, demanding, nagging, dogmatic, manipulate, disrespectful, rationalizer, over-explainer, know-it-all.

9. **Angry or antagonistic**
   Lashes out physically or verbally, screams or curses, quick temper, tantrums, rage, volatile, violent, punitive, unjust punishment, insulting, vindictive, hold mistakes against self or others, withhold affection or presence, sarcastic, child beating, spouse beating, irrational.

10. **Money/work/authority**
    Spendthrift, fear of poverty, materialistic, workaholic, trapped in a job, stressed out, fear of failure, dislike authority, undermines authority, rebel/do the opposite, procrastinate

11. **Resistant or Defensive**
    Resist help or support, need to be right, escape, don't tell me what to do, no one can help me, contrarian, all or nothing, hypocritical, doesn't listen, pessimistic, demand attention, I know best, lazy or unfocused.

How the exercise should now be handled will vary from family to family; some will jump right in, while others will need to carefully develop it over time. But it could be an important step in developing the parent-child bonds.

Once we compile our list, we can ask our spouse to also complete a list and then compare them to see if each of us would suggest some additions. (If this seems hard, we are doing this in preparation to approach our kids for their lists and to compare our lists with theirs, so we want to appear and to be as open as possible.)

Before we ask our kids to fill out their lists, we want to explain to them that we are doing this exercise to build the bonds within our family, the concept of NEDs, how they are passed down, plus sharing a couple of negative patterns we marked down for ourselves.

Hopefully in their lists, both parents and kids will identify some common negative patterns that begin to define NEDs. At the very least, the sharing should help both parents and kids "get out of the box" of self-deception as it was described earlier, so that our own shortcomings don't lead us to focus on the shortcomings in each other. Instead, each family member is taking ownership of their shortcomings, which creates Brother's Keeper relationships within the family where the negative patterns of all are in the open and receive help in a more supportive way.

PEDs Exercise

Our next exercise should try to identify our individual and family PEDs and strengths.

In the book *Character Strengths and Virtues* (Oxford Press, 2004) authors Christopher Peterson and Martin E. P. Seligman took on the monumental task of identifying the positive traits of human beings. They subdivided 24 qualities in 6 categories:

1. **Wisdom and Knowledge**
   Creativity
   Curiosity
   Open-mindedness
   Love of learning
   Perspective and wisdom

2. **Courage**
   Bravery
   Persistence
   Integrity
   Vitality

3. **Humanity**
   Love
   Kindness
   Social intelligence

4. **Justice**
   Active citizenship
   Fairness
   Leadership

5. **Temperance**
   Forgiveness
   Humility
   Prudence
   Self-control

6. **Transcendence**
   Appreciation of beauty and excellence
   Gratitude
   Hope
   Humor
   Spirituality

We again could list these words on a piece of paper, and then spend some time thinking of qualities we could add to the list. After we share the list with our spouse and kids, we as a family could decide what strengths and values best describe our family. We might create a family motto from it.

Another very important exercise is to write a letter to our mother or father, without giving any thought of what we are going to do with the letter after we write it. We are writing it to try to help us release all the deepest feelings we had as a child, to bring harmony between our heart and mind, and live the truth as I referred to it in the introduction. If we truly write it for ourselves, we may be very surprised at the deeper feelings and memories that flow onto the paper.

After we write it, we can throw it away, put it in a drawer, or if the parent is still alive, send it or even visit the parent and read it to him or her. We can also read it to our spouse and kids, which will give them deeper insight into us, further our bonds with them, and encourage them to do the same.

If all this seems a bit too much, it is important to keep in mind that the more we understand our parents, the more we understand ourselves, and the better we are able to let go of them so we can move on with our own lives. And as I indicated above, dealing with our childhood and sharing it with our kids helps us become the growth models our kids can identify with.

To keep this going, the family should plan to have a family meeting from time to time, perhaps even on a regular basis, where each member reports in on what they feel good about in what they are doing in their life, and what they are struggling with. Sometimes these meeting can be short, but at least once a year, there should be an in-depth meeting where each member shares what they hope to accomplish in the coming year, and what they see as potential obstacles.

To summarize, in order to help our kids realize their best and become self-sufficient, we need parent-child bonds and to be accepted as mentors. Since we primarily teach by example, we can accomplish this by sharing our growth, particularly our childhood, with our kids.

Unique Potential

Throughout this book, there have been constant references to unique potential, not only by me, but by other Hyde people as well. With all the work we have done on NEDs and PEDs, readers are now in a much better position to understand the concept.

We are born with a unique potential, as well as a spirit and natural capacity to love. By following our spirit, we find things in life that we do well and that are deeply fulfilling. As we do these things, like the sailboat that must tack into the wind, we will always get closer to our true destination. Thus if we try to pursue those things that are truly fulfilling in life, we are in the process of fulfilling our destiny, which is a product of expressing our unique potential on the paths we take.

But this is only the *nature* part of the unique potential equation, which can be overpowered by the *nurture* side—the powerful influence of our parents and our upbringing. We have seen throughout the book the struggles within families centered around NEDs and adverse childhood experience. How well we—and our parents—are able to deal with these struggles largely determines how much we are able to free our spirit and become open to the development of our unique potential.

Beyond our genes, our families pass on powerful PEDs to us going back generations that can greatly enhance our unique potential. So these powerful PEDs are available to us even if we are adopted.

But generally, the more powerful the PEDs, the more powerful the NEDs—that is, the more we try to accomplish in life, the tougher it gets and the more problems we have. In my case, I think my mother came from a family of strong PEDs, but a family that was darkened by a NED centered on my grandmother's domineering and often-mean alcoholism that my grandfather never confronted, at least publicly.

My mother was one of five daughters who all struggled in life with this NED that affected all of their families and sapped to different degrees how each utilized the PED strength of our family heritage.

I feel very fortunate that I benefitted from my mother's commitment and spirit before she eventually got lost in addiction and insanity, and also that she married Brownlee, my stepfather, a man of high principles, a patriot, and dedicated parent, in spite of his lack of people skills.

I think this nurturing, combined with the help I received in transcending most of my NEDs from Hyde, Al-Anon, Hoffman, and others, enabled me to utilize my deeper PED heritage to support the development of my unique potential.

In 1976, I began to learn about the exceptional character of my great-grandfather John Ebeneezer Warren. I read an *Atlantic Monthly* article he wrote regarding the brutal conditions he endured while interned at Andersonville prison during the Civil War. He ends the article:

> *The war has long been over; its wounds have healed, and its scars are rapidly being obliterated; the principal actors in its scenes are rapidly disappearing from the stage of life, and we, who as boys formed the rank and file of the grand army, are men now, or never will be.*
>
> *I can truthfully say that in spite of the dangers and privations that it brought, in spite even of Andersonville, I have no regrets for the four years or more in which I wore a short artillery jacket and reinforced trousers of good Union blue, and I deem it a privilege to have been permitted to have a hand in the conflict that maintained the Union and brought freedom to the slave.*

This sense of patriotism was further instilled in me by my stepfather, who left Harvard during WWI to join an ambulance corps in France (he refused to kill; only to save lives.) He was awarded the Croix de Guerre by the French for taking an ambulance into no man's land under fire to save a number of French soldiers.

Then in 1988, I discovered in some old papers my mother left me a sermon by my great-grandfather Abel Pottle. It was on the development of character and delivered in a church in Bath, Maine in 1888! It was eerie. As I read his sermons, I realized he had a vision of trying to unite the world's religions. Was this PED the foundation for my vision of trying to change American education?

All this made me realize my life had reflected some of the qualities and standards of these men. I never would have thought that possible in my twenties.

We all have a rich heritage of PEDs in our family background. The only question is how well will we deal with our family NEDs in order to fully utilize those PEDs.

Reaching Out

We should now feel a real sense of empowerment. We have been able to recognize and appreciate the positive qualities of our families, and yet at the same time, fully realize our negative patterns, their source, and our ability to deal with them.

Realizing that our negative patterns were passed down from previous generations enables us to stop beating ourselves up for our shortcomings, appreciate our strengths, while accepting ourselves as a work in progress. This gives us a new-found serenity, while truly making us a model our kids can identify with, look up to and follow.

We should feel the desire to reach out and share what we have learned with other parents and families. This will not only give us that great feeling of making a contribution to others, it actually is the vital step in renewing and augmenting the growth we are making in our own family—embodied in the phrase, "You've got to give it away to get it."

Just as a family benefits from synergy, so does a group of families.

So, to truly pursue parenting and family excellence and solidify them in a culture that is presently sometimes alien to what we are establishing, I urge you to seek to create a group of parents and families to share and create the synergy that has been so meaningful for Hyde parents and families.

If you decide to take this step, there will be a lot of help available to you. There are over five-thousand Hyde alumni parents and there are bound to be some in your area who would be delighted to help you. We could also send you the curriculum materials we use for Hyde parents, and keep you in touch with other groups to help you utilize what they are doing.

These groups would not only provide support to parents and families, but they would be vital in creating a positive peer culture for the kids.

We live in an age when there are many powerful forces—commercial, electronic, and otherwise—who are not sensitive to or who do not recognize the family as the center of our society. Yet family forms the core of our human life experience.

So this is a time when concerned parents need to reach out to other concerned parents to form groups where the family reigns supreme, sending a vital message to their children, and providing them with a more comprehensive preparation for life. It truly does take a village to raise a child, and Hyde Schools and I stand ready to help you in your efforts.

Good Luck!

ACKNOWLEDGEMENTS

After reading this book, it should be clear that my primary teachers in developing it were Hyde families, including my own. What may not be obvious is the wisdom that came from the dedication of Hyde teachers, who work tirelessly to keep the Hyde process at a level of excellence.

I want to pay a special word of thanks to those Hyde families, including my own, who shared their personal stories in the book. This was not an easy task. They not only helped to bring a reality to the power of PEDs and NEDs in our lives, but also how dealing with them strengthens our bonds and mentorships with our children.

Finally I want to thank my editor Cindy Warnick for her dedication and integrity and for making this a much better book. I also want to thank my agent, Laura Yorke, for her help, enthusiasm, and encouragement.

The Gauld-MacMillan-Hurd Family

From left to right: (front row) Wilson and Kayla MacMillan; (second row) Hannah MacMillan, Mahalia Gauld, and Gigi and Don MacMillan; (third row) Laurie and Georgia Hurd, and Joe, Harrison (hidden), Laura, Malcolm and Scout Gauld; (back row) Meddy, Paul and Zach Hurd.

**To learn more about Joe Gauld
and the Hyde Schools,
please visit www.hyde.edu.**